A Stitch in Time

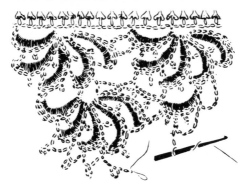

For my niece Gabrielle Warren
and in memory of her grandmother Rose Warren (1890–1975)
whom she so much resembles.

Geoffrey Warren

A Stitch in Time

VICTORIAN AND EDWARDIAN
NEEDLECRAFT

Taplinger Publishing Company
New York

First published in the United States in 1976 by
TAPLINGER PUBLISHING CO., INC.
New York, New York
Copyright © 1976 by Geoffrey Warren
All rights reserved.
Printed in Great Britain

Library of Congress Catalog Card Number 76–12187
ISBN 0–8008–7435–8

Contents

List of illustrations

Introduction

'. . . a useful and ladylike accomplishment . . .'
Knitting, Netting and Crochet   MRS ELIZABETH JACKSON 1845

'Work, work, work with the needle from almost childhood, in the same closed room from morning to night, and not infrequently from night to morning also, is the everlasting routine of the monotonous life of dressmakers.'
Dress as a Fine Art   MRS MERRIFIELD 1854

In 1893 Mrs Masters in her *Book of Needlework* regretted the advent of the 'New Woman' who seemed to be forsaking her time-honoured spheres. Among these was needlecraft which, Mrs Masters foresaw, in time would be the occupation only of invalids. But, to judge by the number of women who, over 80 years later, are still engaged in all sorts of needlecraft her gloomy prognostication was obviously wrong. There has even been a revival of some of the more obscure and often rather difficult old arts such as tatting, macramé and patchwork.

Yet the volume of needlework today is as nothing compared to that produced in the period covered by this book. During it, nearly every home, from palace to cottage, was stuffed with every conceivable object made of, or decorated with, a bewildering number of techniques—not to mention the amount of clothing and accessories embellished in the same way. In this respect, as in so many others, the average Victorian and Edwardian had little idea of when to stop. Nowadays we have more restraint, less time and our ideas of what is necessary or 'tasteful' have radically changed. The fact that so much needlework was done, however, does mean that it is still possible to find, often at surprisingly little cost, many good examples of Victorian and Edwardian work from crochet tablecloths to beaded bags.

Not only are we astonished by the volume of such work but by the number of objects, many of them now obsolete, upon which it was thought fit to apply needlework. Today no one would dream of embroidering (even if such things were common) a cigar case with silks or seeds in flower shapes. As not many men now use cut-throat razors there is little need for a shaving 'book' consisting of cloth 'pages' and a cover of embroidered perforated cardboard. We neither use nor embroider bell-pulls or footstools. Nor do we decorate paperweights or picture frames in satin-stitch, let alone sermon cases, key-baskets, visiting-card trays, fern presses, sachets in which to keep Christmas cards, log baskets, letter racks or bird-cage covers—to name but a few of the artefacts which symbolise a lifestyle so at variance with our own.

There are, however, many items of Victorian and Edwardian needlework which we are rediscovering, reappreciating and using as originally intended or putting to new uses. Crocheted, be-laced or broderie anglaise curtains find favour as do the elaborately tuck-ed and frilled nightdresses and nightshirts. Wool-worked bell-pulls and the beaded covering of trays are used to decorate cushion-covers; scraps of patchwork or lace are put under glass to make coffee-table tops. Crochet and lace-edged pillow-cases, sheets and bedspreads are again popular as are even little mats; although the most bizarre—those made in imitation of flowers and foliage by winding wool round wire frames—are unlikely to be revived, even if they are still to be found.

From which it may be gathered that this book will, in the main, be concerned with what was made in and for the average middle-class home by the average middle-class 'lady' as well as those of the 'lower orders'. These countless, now mostly unknown women, although they could not help being influenced to some extent by artists, decorators and art and fashion movements, happily went their own untroubled and largely unaesthetic way.

1 'Good' and 'bad' taste

'. . . the Great Exhibition in Hyde Park is of all things the best cal-
culated to advance our National Taste . . .'
ART-JOURNAL SPECIAL ISSUE, THE CRYSTAL PALACE ILLUSTRATED
CATALOGUE 1851

Although, when considering the standard of domestic taste from
about 1830 onwards, too much emphasis is often given to the influence of 'great' artists and designers, we cannot completely ignore
them or the various artistic movements and changes of fashion
which occurred in this country between 1837 when Queen Victoria ascended the throne and 1910 when her son Edward VII
vacated it. The Crystal Palace Exhibition of 1851 reflected the taste
of the day and was to influence it for nearly the rest of the century.

Just what this taste was is best summed up, not by present-day
hindsight and detachment, but by two contemporary critics. The
main contention was that the exhibition showed nothing new—in
taste that is, not in inventions, of which there were plenty.
Although it was the gathering together from all over the world of
what was considered the best in art it was, in fact, only an assem-
blage of what one critic called 'archeologism run wild'. It ran
'helter-skelter after Classic, Gothic, Morresque and almost every
other excellence hitherto attained'. The same opinion was voiced
by Owen Jones in his *Grammar of Ornament* of 1858 in which he
deplored the 'unfortunate tendency of our time to be content with
copying. . . .' Not only copying, but haphazard mixing, so that
any object from a building to a footstool could combine an un-
comfortable and often grotesque combination of styles.

And this was nowhere more evident than in the English section
of 'Tapestry, Floor-Cloths, Lace and Embroidery'. As this was the
height of the Berlin wool work craze—what we now call 'tapestry' work (for a fuller explanation see chapter four)—there were
many pictures, curtains and dress accessories executed in wool,
copied from squared designs. Like traditional Texans, the Victorians of the 1850s seem to have been impressed by size for its own
sake. A contemporary observed that in the Embroidery Section
'the exhibitors seemed to have been under the delusion that the size

A Victorian lady at work on, and
surrounded by, many examples of
the objects to which she could
apply her needle, 1901

13

of a piece of work, and the number of years that must have been wasted over it (automatically) earned it a place in the exhibition'.

Another critic and one who was to have some positive success in 'reforming' this state of affairs was John Ruskin, critic, artist and writer. Only seventeen when he visited the exhibition, Ruskin was so appalled by what he saw that he refused to complete the exhausting tour, declaring that everything was 'wonderfully ugly'. Instead, he advocated a return to Medievalism, in design and craftsmanship. The Pre-Raphaelite Brotherhood, founded in 1848 and which included such artists as Rossetti, Millais and Burne-Jones (the last to design much embroidery), had already come to the same conclusion. They tried to return to what seemed to them the ideal civilisation which had existed in Europe before Raphael. Ruskin not only made many written attempts to reform taste in this direction but also tried, personally, to reach the 'people'. His encouragement of local crafts in the Lake District (further explored in chapter four) was only one of his activities. He taught at a Working Men's College where he attempted to instil creativity in his listeners who were told not to rely on the machine which he so much loathed. He ignored the fact that most people do not have it in them to be creative and are only too glad to rely on this gift in others, and that the machine was there to stay.

This mistake was also made by Ruskin's disciple, William Morris, artist, designer, craftsman, writer and socialist who founded his own handicraft firm in 1861. Morris's other mistake was to produce hand made objects which were far too expensive for the poor he was trying to reach. In 1855 he had already experimented with an embroidery frame made to his own design and using specially dyed wools. Although a Medievalist, he was no mere imitator as most of his tapestries, wallpapers and embroideries etc, bear his personal stamp and, whether he liked it or not, much commercial and machine made domestic articles were influenced by his style.

Morris's designs were all stylised interpretations of natural forms; not for him the almost three-dimensional cabbage roses and lilies so beloved of Berlin wool and bead workers which Lady Marion Alford, in her *Needlework as Art* of 1866, called 'vegetable forms . . . reminiscent of a kitchen garden in a tornado'. In one of his lectures Morris told his listeners that 'it is a quite delightful idea to cover a piece of linen cloth with roses, jonquils and tulips done quite natural with the needle. . . .' He reminded them of the fact that as they were using beautiful materials they must make the most of them and not forget that they were 'gardening with silk and gold thread'.

At his famous Red House in Bexley Heath, Morris designed and executed all the furniture and fittings. His wife Jane embroidered brightly coloured flowers on to blue serge hangings for the master bedroom and, practicing what he preached, Morris joined her and their two young daughters in this work. The younger daughter, May, was later to become an embroideress of some note. One of Morris's techniques was to simulate woven work by covering the material with close-laid stitches; another was to embroider linen shapes with gold and silk and then appliqué them on a heavier woollen ground.

In 1878 Morris & Co took an order for a set of friezes for the dining room of Routon Grange designed by Philip Webb. Burne-Jones was given the job and produced a series of scenes from Chaucer's *Roumaunt of the Rose* to be worked with wools, silk and gold thread on linen. It took the owner, Lady Margaret Bell and her daughters eight years to complete—and one can only hope that they weren't heartily sick of it by the end. Burne-Jones collaborated with Morris on many more designs; the former using his out-line technique, the latter, his filled-in one.

If Morris and his followers were out of touch his successors such as the 'Art' Needleworkers and the Aesthetes (whose motto was 'Art for Art's Sake') were, on the whole, more realistic. These latter were a particular phenomenon of the 1870s and '80s who, in extreme cases 'looked at a lily for breakfast' and sat up all night with a dying daffodil. The men wore velvet knickerbockers and the women loose gowns covered in even looser embroidery.

But they, the Arts and Crafts Movement and like Guilds, paved the way for the Art Nouveau Movement, which can be considered the only truly original art form the Victorians produced. It was basically a revolt against the very pastiche for which the Great Exhibition of 1851 had stood. Its premises: purity of line, nature as an inspiration, fitness for purpose, acceptance of the machine and that a unity of design should be strived for in every domestic art, are still in evidence today.

Even the London shop, Liberty, founded in 1875, did much to foster this 'new art', particularly with its fabrics and embroideries. Many art journals and magazines were great supporters of Art Nouveau. In particular *The Studio,* first published in 1893, which reported on its exhibitions at home and abroad, encouraged its ideas and ideals in every way. In 1903 it published an article called 'Some Experiments in Embroidery'. The author (like Morris) was against naturalism, shading and the imitation of painting, and asked if it was necessary to compete with the painter what could be achieved by the needle? Despite this awareness of the new ways it is salutary to note that even *The Studio* showed examples of art and craft which still bore strong traces of 1851 pastiche.

1 An unusual work-table made in the form of a miniature 'dumb waiter'. Each tier edged with elaborately embroidered and decorated valances, 1876

2 'Ladies'-and others

'. . . a woman must be domestic. Her heart must be at home. She . . .
must find pleasure as well as her occupation in the sphere which is
assigned to her.'

WOMAN IN HER SOCIAL AND DOMESTIC CHARACTER   Mrs John
Sandford, 1837

By 1837 when Queen Victoria came to the throne the Industrial
Revolution was in full, uncheckable swing. As well as giving new
work to thousands of virtual slaves in factories and mines, it also
created an unprecedentedly large class of well-off women with too
much time on their hands, who were as much slaves to their condition as their poorer sisters.

In this very year, Mrs John Sandford published a comment on
the lot of this class called *Woman in her Social and Domestic Character*.
It is, ostensibly, a plea for the further education of 'ladies' but in
fact it does much to define and support the status quo. Mrs Sandford considered her sex incapable of being artistic as it 'lacked the
originality and strength requisite for the sublime' and incapable of
greatness as littleness of mind was its peculiarity. As women, in her
opinion, were only busy about little things and vexed by little
cares the only effort they made by way of occupation was to read a
novel or work a flower in needlework.

Although apparently in favour of some sort of emancipation,
Mrs Sandford was vague as to how this was to be achieved; while
admitting that there must be more to life than music, drawing and
needlework, she offered no practical alternatives. So what else
were the poor things to do but work a flower? No wonder that
they produced such prodigious quantities of often useless handicrafts from cork pictures to embroidered coal-scuttle mats, which
represent not only hours of boredom but a terrible waste—not
only of time but of human intelligence.

Someone who was gifted above the average and who naturally
rebelled against what was expected of a 'lady' in this century, was
Florence Nightingale. In her autobiographical unpublished novel
Cassandra written in 1852 (two years before she was released by the
Crimean War) she painted a picture of a typical dreary morning
which leisured ladies filled by 'sitting around a little table in the

drawing-room, looking at prints, doing worsted work, and reading little books'. Many women must, of course, have enjoyed such occupations and indeed have been grateful for them—they could not *all* be Florence Nightingales. Their leisure work filled in time and for those with little or no talent for anything else, such ladylike accomplishments solved the problem of having to think as well as serving to set them firmly apart from the dreadful mass of females who had to *earn* their living.

More realistic than Mrs Sandford and more in line with Miss Nightingale were the views expressed in *The English Women's Journal* which, in its 1858 June issue, published an article called 'Female Education in the Middle Classes'. 'The whole social condition of women,' it begins, 'during these fifty years, has undergone a thorough revolution.' Mrs Sandford had voiced the opinion that housewifely duties were 'inelegant'. But as *The Journal* pointed out, without these tasks which had kept heads and hands busy, their owners were a prey to that 'curse of middle-class existence, that death in life, ennuie'.

In 1851, out of a population of about six million women over twenty, one half had no place in non-domestic industry and remained at home as wives and daughters. The upper classes did not much care if they were idle, the lower *had* to work and the middle was left in a vacuum. And what better to fill it with than the branches of needlecraft open to them—many of which were, one feels, only created for this purpose.

The author of the article in *The Women's Journal* did not think this enough. She considered that 'days thus frittered away . . . lose all the charm of periodic activity, of that wondrous play of action and reaction in which the animate Creation exists and delights'.

But things were different for whose who, from necessity or because of their 'lower' station in life, were forced to spend all day and often half the night in 'periodical activity' which can have had little charm about it, let alone delight. However arduous, boring, time-wasting and corrosive middle-class ladies' occupations may have been, they were nothing to the sheer drudgery they meant for thousands of others.

As a means of earning living, needlecraft was appallingly ill-paid and often crippling to health. As well as being employed in factories and workshops thousands did piece-work at home. In Ayrshire and Western Scotland agents travelled around miner's cottages where the wives and daughters were only too glad to take in needlework to eke out their menfolk's miserable wages. The embroidery done by these cottagers (often called Ayrshire work, see chapter four) was particularly intricate as it was executed in fine cotton on muslin and as it was often sewn by candlelight it

2 '. . . Ladylike
accomplishment . . .'

took its toll in human suffering. Some of the poor creatures had to
resort to bathing their tired eyes in whisky which, although painful, allowed them to work more easily for a few more hours. For
this sort of work in 1851 such workers, if skilled, could earn 10s a
week, if only average then only 1s to 6d. Conditions were no
better in the south. During 1844, out of 669 patients admitted to
the North London Ophthalmic Institution, 81 of them were poor
needlewomen whose eyes had been severely injured by too long a
'devotion' to their work. Even in 1869 wages in Scotland, even for
the most expert, were only 10d to 2s a day—a day which lasted
from seven in the morning to eleven or twelve at night.

Warehouse seamstresses on piece-work in London in 1859 could
earn from 6s to £1 a week but their work varied with the seasons—to as little as 5s a week in lean times. During some weeks the
best workers could not earn even this and 'inferior' ones only 2s to

3 '. . . the toil!—oh, the toil!'

3s. In 1859 a seamstress widow and three of her four children were found dead of starvation in a garret.

The Women's Journal was rightly indignant at such a state of affairs. '. . . the toil!—oh, the toil! Not for a fair day's work do they realise these amounts—by a fair day's work, I mean that a woman shall sew unremittingly ten hours, not *twenty*.' *The Journal* goes on to say: 'Who can describe the state of mind and body consequent on having sewn twenty hours a day for six days? No one, yet there are thousands who know *exactly*. Could the multitudes composing this wretched class be collected into one host, what appalling aggregate of misery would the scene present!'

A different sort of slave to needlework was the 'distressed gentlewoman'. This class would include 'ladies' who, for one reason or another—being widowed, spinsters, poor relations or victims of their fathers' or husbands' sudden loss of income—had to work for a living, or at least to supplement what little living they had. They found themselves in the same plight as the 'lower orders' they so often despised, but usually without that strata's age-long knowhow, resilience and acceptance of its lot.

The only 'respectable' employment for such women was to become a governess, a schoolmistress or a companion, although even these jobs were somewhat despised. But nothing was so looked down on as being 'in trade'. The stigma which society attached to this is one of the great hypocrisies of the Victorian age. Although many 'ladies and gentlemen' derived their incomes, their homes, their servants and their status from this very source, to *admit* to being in trade was a fate, if not worse than death, then at least its equal. To be fair, many a sheltered 'lady' spent her whole life unaware that her husband, father or other male member of her family, either in the present or the past, were owners of, or investors in, commercial enterprises.

For every unsupported 'needy lady' in 1800 it was reckoned that by the middle of the century they could be counted in dozens; by the end, in thousands. It is not surprising, therefore, that a number of societies and organisations was set up to sell needlework executed by these desperate women. For those who dreaded it being known that they were engaged in trade, several subterfuges were resorted to. 'The Ladies' Work Society', founded in about 1875 to 'provide employment for gentlewomen whose circumstances render it necessary that they should employ their leisure time remuneratively' disguised their members' names by numbers.

'The Ladies' Crystal Palace Stall' entitled ladies to exhibit twelve articles at a time and ensured *strictest* confidence with regard to names and addresses of members. A Mrs Elliot, who founded a 'Work Society' owing to her home at the Vicarage, Horncastle, being broken up firmly announced that no letters would be answered unless accompanied by *three* stamps.

In 1882 Mrs Sharpe of Shrewsbury, who claimed to be a gentlewoman, advertised that she was prepared to introduce an 'Entirely Novel and Beautiful Trimming composed of either pearl, cut, black, gold, steel or any other description of beads', but to hide from her neighbours that she was in trade, she stated that she would accept no postcards.

Societies had to be careful as to the 'standing' of prospective members. 'The Association for the Sale of Work of Ladies of Limited Means' which was 'intended solely for gentlewomen by birth' required that a prospective member be proposed by a bona fidé one; as did 'The Working Ladies' Guild' which was a 'very extensive Society, organised by a number of influential ladies and gentlemen'. 'The Gentlewomen's Self-Help Institute' was very particular: not only had its members to be of gentle birth but needed two letters of recommendation, one of which had to be from a clergyman.

Ladies had, of course, to pay for the privilege of belonging to such organisations. 'The Royal Charitable Repository' of Leamington, which claimed to be the oldest of such institutions, asked one guinea yearly membership plus 1d in the shilling commission: 5s was the usual entrance fee plus 10s annual subscription. 'The Ladies' Industrial Society' charged an entrance fee of 5s and took 1d in the shilling commission. 'The Ladies' Work Society' took as much as 2d to 2½d in the shilling.

The standard of work was also important. The Bristol 'Depot for the Sale of Work by Ladies of Limited Means' required a specimen of work as proof and they rejected anything unsaleable or badly made. 'The Ladies' Work Society' of Liverpool also required a high standard sample from prospective members so that it could be 'quietly and advantageously' disposed of. (Which sounds more like getting rid of an unwanted child than a piece of needlework.) 'Mrs Geyselman's Depot for Ladies' Work' in Torquay laid down that 'all plain work be hand sewn, well executed as well as being pretty and useful'. A low price was advised to induce a 'ready sale'.

It is hard to discover what these distressed gentlewomen actually earned. Although by no means an indication of what was paid to the embroideress herself we do know what the 'Royal School of Art Needlework' charged its customers for embroidered work in 1880. A long curtain border cost about £2 10s. From £2 2s to £10 was paid for a linen or silk sofa-back and ladies' tennis aprons cost from £1 5s to £3 10s. A tea-cosy or cloth was only 16s 6d but a folding screen could be as much as £100.

One of the most interesting books on this subject and one written in an unpatronising and kind tone was *Needlework for Ladies for Pleasure and Profit* published in 1880 under the pen-name of 'Dorinda'. Her sensible advice was addressed not so much to those 'necessitous' ladies, as to those who wished to make some pin-money out of the work done during their leisure hours. She ignored the stigma of the word 'trade' and frankly admitted that selling was part of the business and gave practical advice as to possible commercial outlets.

Despite the fact that so many journals, magazines and books produced a prodigious number of patterns for such things, 'Dorinda' maintained that there was no outlet for what she called 'old-fashioned fancy-work', because 'fine art needlework' had taken its place. She considered that these small, easily soiled knick-knacks were useless and a waste of time to make. (Perhaps too many homes had more than enough of them already for ladies to want to *buy* any more.) The author advised her readers not to be too reliant on patterns and was insistent that all work 'must keep pace with the times and . . . be up to standard'. She suggested that a 'reasonable' price be asked, based on the cost of the materials, the time taken (usually five or six hours a day) and added that on *no account* must more be asked than the normal shop price. In tune with many of the Societies she stressed that work must be well-made and 'really' useful for dresses or furniture. She said that the larger the article, the better chance it had of selling, and the standard had to be high to avoid the disappointment of having a parcel of work returned 'Unsaleable'. Oh, the heartache such labelled parcels must have caused those ladies who, often in strict privacy and by devious means, had painstakingly made and embroidered many items which they had anxiously hoped would make them a little money, if not a living.

Not surprisingly, 'Dorinda' advised that knitted and crocheted articles sold well in the winter. She told her readers that many London firms were willing to give out a good deal of work which included trousseaux, layettes, ladies' and children's 'wearing apparel', stocking embroidery, beading on net for bonnet crowns and lace flounces, muslin and lace work. Such items were, apparently, 'fairly well' (whatever that meant) paid but as it was on a strictly business basis, ladies were advised to send in their order on the *very* day for which it was promised—which must have meant more than a little burning of the midnight oil. The anonymous author also advised lady workers not to hesitate to take examples of their work to local 'fancy repositories' in their own neighbourhoods and even not to be afraid of publicity. A magazine called *The Bazaar* devoted two or three columns to work done by amateurs. It also ran a useful 'Exchange and Mart' section which enabled ladies to dispose of articles with 'Ease, Economy and Expedition'. Other papers such as *Myra's, Sylvia's Home Journal* and *Weldon's* ran similar columns. 'Dorinda', safe behind her pseudonym, even went so far as to advise her hard-up ladies to make a careful study of shop windows as this would repay study and anything new and pretty could be copied.

3 Patronised and patronising

'The Queen and her Ladies-in-waiting
* Sat in the window and sewed.'*

THE WIND IN THE WILLOWS   Kenneth Grahame, 1908

In 1847 Queen Adelaide, widow of William IV was still alive and living in retirement at Bently Priory, although she was to die there two years later. Mrs Owen, in her *The Illuminated Book of Needlework* of 1847 informed her readers that few charitable bazaars in the country were not 'enriched' by the Queen Dowager's work, for which a high price was 'gladly' paid. Mrs Owen somewhat tactlessly added that this was not for the intrinsic worth of the work but because it had been 'wrought by a hand which every Englishwoman had learned to respect and love'.

Another royal hand which was not always respected and loved was that of Queen Victoria who knitted 'comforts' for the troops during the Crimean War. But she was furious when she learned that they had been given to the officers and not to the men as she had intended. She also encouraged the revival of various branches of needlework by ordering the christening robe for the Princess Royal in 1840 from Ayrshire and embroidered curtains for Windsor Castle from Mrs Hart's 'Ladies' School' in Donegal in 1886.

The Queen and other royal ladies graciously allowed books on needlecraft to be dedicated to them and gave their patronage to various societies. One of the first of these was 'The Royal School of Art Needlework' (it dropped the 'Art' in 1922) which was open only to those who could claim 'poverty, gentle birth, and sufficient capacity to enable them to support themselves and be educated to each others'. It was founded in 1872 by Lady Welby with the aim of 'restoring . . . ornamental Needlework to the high place it once held among the decorative Arts'. The School researched, learned lost stitches and had wools and silks dyed in 'beautiful tints'. Lady Welby was lucky to gain Princess Christian of Schleswig-Holstein (the fifth child of Queen Victoria) as President and active helper. By 1875 the Queen herself was patron—later to

23

be joined by the Prince and Princess of Wales. No Society could hope for higher patronage. As Vice-President, the School appointed Lady Marion Alford, author of *Needlework as Art* published in 1886, from which much of this information is taken. Her report of 1873 (which was printed by 'The Lady's Printing Press' founded for the 'Tuition and Employment of Necessitous Gentlewomen') stated that orders in the 'executive' department for the past year amounted to 405, and those in the 'prepared' as much as 1,165. The first department dealt with work done at the School, the other with that sent out for working. This would consist of a traced design with part of the work begun and enough materials to finish the job (which does not sound much of an incentive to the 'creativity' so much advocated by the School and the Art Needlework people). Ladies could supply their own materials, but before being sent, dresses had to be cut out and tacked with lines marked for the embroidery.

The School was divided into three workrooms. One was in the charge of an 'accomplished lady' who overlooked the execution of work from the most delicate to the most 'effective'. Another room was devoted to gold and appliqué work, overseen by another 'lady' who had studied in the 'best Foreign Schools'. The third 'artistic' room was given over to work designed by William Morris, Burne-Jones, Walter Crane and others.

Such was the School's standing that it was able to persuade these important artists to design for them. Even so, a book published by the School in 1880, written by Mr L. Higgen and edited by Lady Alford gives sadly little evidence of originality. It is illustrated with twenty-two plates, some in colour, most in black-and-white. Even designs by William Morris (a sofa-back and wall-hanging), Burne-Jones (a wall panel called 'Maria' in his out-line technique) and Walter Crane (a wall-screen and a panel representing the Four Elements) are pretty feeble. Far from being original, Walter Crane's contribution is clearly Renaissance-inspired and an anonymous design for a border in appliqué work firmly states that it is copied from an early Italian original.

In 1875 an affiliated school was formed with the far from modest title: 'A Higher School of Art'. In the following year the Royal School had such a success at the Philadelphia Centennial Exhibition that many embroidery schools were started in major cities throughout America, most of the teachers coming from the parent school. This went from strength to strength: Silver Medal at the Paris International Exhibition of 1878; branches and agencies all over the British Isles, so that their influence on 'Art' needlework was quite considerable and widespread. The Duchess of Northumberland, the Countess of Ravensworth and the Countess Percy,

Lady Ridley, gave the School their support.

Oh, how much such schools and societies relied on noble, if not royal patronage! Although the Royal School had beaten all others by having the Sovereign as chief patron. 'The Bradford Art Needlework Society' was successful in persuading the Princess of Wales to be its patron. 'The Ladies' Work Society' managed to secure the presidency of HRH Princess Louise; 'The Society for Promoting Female Welfare' had the Duchess of Connaught (wife of Arthur, Queen Victoria's seventh child) as patron and later—in 1910—Princess Marie-Louise, grand-daughter of the Queen. Other societies had to make do with less exalted personages. 'The Royal Charitable Repository' (despite its name) was under a conductress and others had only managers, treasurers, superintendents and secretaries—acting or honorary.

As well as lending their names, many of these titled women gave active support. Princess Louise (sixth daughter of Queen Victoria) in 1877 even designed a *portiere* for the State Rooms of Waterhouse's new Town Hall in Manchester. It had a deep border of dark blue on which sunflowers—the symbol of the Aesthetic Movement—were appliquéd. In 1893 the Marchioness of Lorne prepared many of the designs executed by 'The Ladies' Work Society' and even a noble lord, Viscount Dillon, set up several schools to encourage knitting on his estate at Loughglyn.

The Needlecraft Monthly (1907–1913) ran a regular feature called 'Noble Needleworkers'. In 1908 it featured Viscountess Hood who specialised in bedspreads and quilts, Lady Cecile Goff who

4 A Victorian mahogany work-table with hinged top, filled with needlework accessories, c 1840

was 'still' using Jacobean designs (it is not clear if this was intended as a compliment or a rebuke) and Lady Majorie Manners who was responsible for a linen sachet and a bedspread. But the prize for noble endeavour must surely go to Lady Viola who announced that she was about to embark on copying the whole of the Bayeux Tapestry in filet lace. As she devoted only 'odd moments' to her work, she calculated that it would take her five years. Alas, I can find no record that she achieved her gargantuan ambition.

Many ladies, titled or not, gave encouragement to their tenants by founding or reviving home needlework industries. Such a one was 'The Fisherton de la Mere Industry' in Wiltshire which was founded in 1890 by Mrs Arthur Newell to give employment to both sexes and all ages. Mrs Newell concentrated on the technique of counting stitches on evenly woven linen on the lines of Elizabethan tent stitch work. Lady Lillian Weymess and Miss Weymess (later Lady Henry Grosvenor) in the 1880s founded 'The Castle School' in East Fifeshire as employment for the local poor, as well as the 'Weymess School of Needlework'. Concerned by the unemployment caused by the Donegal famines of the 1880s Mrs Ernest Hart appealed for funds to encourage local weaving and knitting. With the money raised she started a school for village children. Not only did she help the 'lower' classes but 'ladies of culture and distinction who were starving like peasants'—sixty to eighty of them, in fact. One imagines that any scruples they might have had about being 'in trade' were soon lost when an empty stomach was experienced.

A number of needlecraft schools were founded in Ireland. Waterford School of Art had fifteen students of embroidery in 1897 and the oddly (although probably only too aptly) named 'Congested District's Board' founded two such schools at Ardar. One taught crochet, the other, embroidery and drawn-work. Some designs were supplied by the workers themselves who could have had little or no training. They were, however, overseen by Miss Albina Collins of Kinsale who had been a National Scholar at the Royal College of Art in London.

Ballnaglerach School, with sixteen workers, made torchon pillow lace and Moneygold of Country Sligo produced crochet work under expert teachers. The 'District's Board' encouraged these workers who, starting at 3s, 5s, 6s, or 7s a week had their wages raised to 4s, 6s 6d and 8s provided they attended regularly. To make sure of this these schools were frequently inspected—which emphasises the Victorian belief that the poor were only so because they were lazy.

The Crossmaglen School was ambitious in that it taught Carrickmacross lace work (known in Ireland since 1820 it was either a form of Brussels lace or a Guipure), appliqué on net and other branches of needlework usually reserved for the 'better' classes. Dublin could boast an Embroidery School run on the lines of the Royal School in London. Here many gentlewomen worked alongside the less genteel and provided a large proportion of the output. There was also the 'Metropolitan School of Art' where pillow lace, Carrickmacross and white linen embroidery were taught; this school, sensibly, had connection with the trade. The 'Lace Depot of Ireland' was very helpful to such schools; being closely allied to the Irish Industries Association it could report very satisfactory sales.

There were also home-based concerns such as the Garryhill Embroidery Industry with two or three workers to each cottage. This was founded by Lady Duncannon and continued for some time under her supervision.

Irish convents were long famed for their excellent needlecraft. Although a great deal of the work was done by nuns or novices, convents were often centres of work for their surrounding areas and the 1890s saw a revival of such classes held in these religious houses. At the 'Presentation Convent' at Kilkenny there was a workroom where Limerick lace and cut linen work, embroidery and torchon pillow lace were taught, the designs being bought from students of the Waterford and Cork Schools of Art. There was a workroom for outside workers at the Convent of Mercy at Clonakily where training was given in the art of coloured embroidery and drawn-work; there were art classes teaching various types of needlecraft at the Convent of Mercy at Ennis and Loretto Convent at Dalkey.

However well intentioned, genuinely concerned and anxious to help those less well off than themselves were the founders of such Societies, Schools and Industries, we cannot escape the fact that there was a patronising strain behind these enterprises. Apart from the fact that convents had a vested interest, there was also a strong insistence on the importance of religion. Typical of the Victorian attitude to this subject were the opinions expressed by Mrs Owen in her *Illuminated Book of Needlework* of 1847. Although glad to note that needlework was being taught in Central, National and other schools for the instruction of the poor and that such schools were even attached to factories, Mrs Owen expressed the heartfelt hope that such teaching would not 'in the smallest iota' interfere with the learning of the catechism which was of such 'vital importance to the future well-being of girls in the lower station in life'. One suspects that Mrs Owen was thinking not only of their well-being but that this religious instruction would keep a much needed labour-force securely in its ill paid 'place'.

4 By hand

'. . . fair fingers ply the needle, either for ornamental or useful purposes . . .'

TREASURES OF NEEDLEWORK   Mrs Warren and Mrs Pullan, 1855

Caulfield's and Seward's *Dictionary of Needlework* first published in 1882 listed hundreds of techniques and stitches—and these were by no means all which were in use during the nineteenth century. To enumerate even a quarter of them, however briefly, would swamp any book. The best that can be done is to describe the most usual—if not always the most easy—which were available to the average or adventurous Victorian and Edwardian needlewoman.

White work

Ayrshire work   This was one of the most beautiful of embroideries bequeathed by the eighteenth century (Plates 5 and 66). It originated from this part of Scotland but also from its West Coast and from Ireland. Its heyday lasted from about 1795 to the late 1850s.

It was fine white embroidery worked on muslin, often embellished with needlepoint fillings. It can be recognised by its incredible fineness and delicacy, a high standard of design, finish and technique which was rarely equalled in any other branch of nineteenth-century needlework.

Although principally a cottage industry it was first organised in Glasgow and Paisley in about 1800, although by 1835 there was strong competition from Ireland. In 1857 the Glasgow firm of Samuel R. & Thomas Brown was employing about 2,000 men and women, whereas from 20 to 30,000 female peasants were working in this industry on the West Coast of Ireland alone. Ayrshire work was exported to England from France, Germany, Russia and the United States.

The designs were mainly floral, so much so that peasants selling them on the roads, offered their 'flowerings'. But other motifs such as rustic implements, animals and people were also popular.

Mountmellick   Even while it was flourishing, Ayrshire work was,

5 Ayrshire-style work. The centre of a small muslin cloth with pillow-lace insertions, c 1850

6 Mountmellick work. A nightdress case, the embroidery carried out in satin, stem and buttonhole stitches, French and bullion knots. Made during the 1890s revival of this work

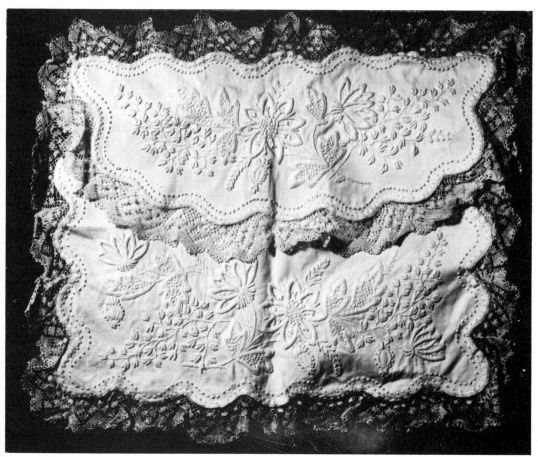

by about 1830, already being supplemented by another less complicated white work, which was introduced from Mountmellick in Queen's County in Ireland. It was stronger and more dramatic than Ayrshire, having a pronounced raised effect achieved by sewing various thicknesses of cotton one over the other (Plate 6). The motifs were also mostly floral, with a tendency for baskets of flowers and fruit as well as many geometrical designs. It was in decline by the late 1870s and Caulfield's *Dictionary* makes no mention of it although there was a revival in about 1887.

Broderie Anglaise   This was a competitor to both the previous techniques and survives today, although it is now mostly machine made. When it first appeared in the 1840s it was given capital letters, as befitted a foreign name, but as the century progressed it was given small ones, indicating that it had become part of the English language. Consisting of holes cut out of muslin, cotton or linen, the art lay in making them, and the buttonhole stitches which framed them, as regular as possible. Round or oval holes were the most usual (Plate 7) but triangular ones were also successfully achieved. A scalloped, buttonhole-edged border was the usual way of finishing off any garment or object decorated wholly or in part with this technique.

Cut-work   The *Dictionary* calls cut-work a form of needlepoint lace but it is, in fact, more generally used to refer to any technique—like broderie anglaise—where holes are made, with the difference that in cut-work these holes are joined by 'bars'. It was worked in a number of ways; chief among them being 'Richelieu Guipure', often referred to as only 'Richelieu' work (Plates 8, 56 and 57), or 'Renaissance Embroidery'. It was based on fourteenth- and sixteenth-century examples but that worked in the nineteenth and early twentieth centuries was far less fine. The 'bars' were

7 Broderie anglaise. Most of the holes are oval-shaped in an unusual Paisley pattern. From the hem of a cotton christening robe, c 1860

8 Richelieu work on linen. Further embellished with running stitches. From a pillow-case, c 1890

usually worked in buttonhole stitch over threads, *before* the holes were cut and the material was often further embellished by embroidery or running stitches.

Laces

Real or pillow lace, worked with bobbins, does not come within the scope of this book, but many lace-like effects (some already mentioned) made by the needle, do qualify. The *Dictionary* devotes at least twenty pages to the subject so that it is possible here to touch on only a few of the most important ones.

Guipure d'Art   Also known as 'Filet Broderie' and 'Irish Broderie' this was one of the most popular. To make it, one needed a wire frame covered round the edge with flannel or ribbon, a wooden netting 'mesh', an ivory netting needle, long blunt embroidery needles and fine and coarse linen thread. Simple netting stitch was first made and then oversewn with a number of other stitches from simple buttonhole to the more complicated '*Point d'Esprit*', '*Point Croise*' and many more. Stars, crosses, flowers and leaves were the most usual designs.

Greek Lace   This was also known as 'Hedebo' or 'Ruskin Work', the latter from the fact that John Ruskin, moved by the plight of

9 Greek or Ruskin work. A square of this lace is inserted into a linen pin-cushion and backed with a piece of printed cotton, c 1890

the poor in the Lake District of England, founded the Ruskin Linen Industry there in 1884 and encouraged the use of this stitch. He had been inspired by the work done in fifteenth-century Venice which was a form of cut-work, using over-casting, buttonhole, satin and backstitches as well as drawn-work to achieve a complicated lace-like effect (Plate 9).

Net Embroidery This also resembled lace and was worked on hand or machine-made net—that from Brussels being considered the best. A variety of designs could be worked on it, using darning, satin and buttonhole stitches (Plates 10, 29, 61 and 69).

Drawn-work 'Dorinda' in her *Needlework for Ladies for Pleasure and Profit* of 1883 dismissed this work with the comment that it was 'tedious' and required great patience. Looking at examples and original patterns one can see what she meant. Weldon's published a series (starting in 1885) called *Practical Drawn Thread Work* and in 1901 *Butterick* put out *The Art of Drawn Work*. This volume takes the amateur step by step to the 'climax of the master'. So complicated and elaborate are all the possibilities of drawing threads, joining them, oversewing them etc, it is a wonder that anyone ever stayed the course. The art was known as early as the twelfth century when it was called *Opus Tiratum* but later by such diverse names as Hambourg Point, Indian Work, Mexican Drawn Work and '*Broderie de Nancy*'. It can be seen in many seventeenth-century English, German and Russian samplers where some of the work is

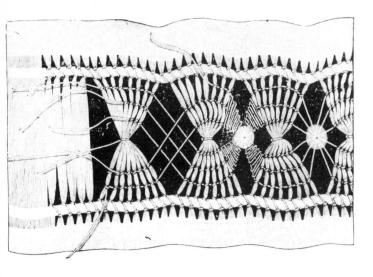

so fine that it requires a magnifying glass in order to appreciate it properly. Later examples, although much coarser, are often incredibly complicated (Plates 11 and 58). Drawn-work lapsed in popularity during the beginning of the nineteenth century but saw a big revival in the '80s.

Berlin work

When Miss A. Lambert in her *Handbook of Needlework* of 1843 made the observation that 'Berlin patterns . . . have contributed more towards the advancement of needlework in the present day, than any improvement that has of late years been introduced into the art', she was voicing a generally held opinion. So popular and universal was it at this time that it was often regarded as synonymous with embroidery. Mrs Owen in 1847 referred to Berlin work as 'tapestry' and went on to say that it was 'certainly the most useful kind of ornamental needlework' which had 'usurped the place of the various other embroideries which from time to time engrossed the leisure moments of the fair'. Along with Miss Lambert and other contemporaries (as well as many people today) she erroneously refers to this work—*hand-stitched* on canvas—as 'tapestry', when that technique is made only on a loom. Berlin work was (and in its modern guise of printed canvasses executed in tent or cross stitch still is) only an *imitation* of true tapestry in the English sense and should be referred to as needlepoint as indeed it is in America (Plates 12, 13, 32, 34, 35, 39, 51, 52, 62, 77 and 90).

In about 1805 a Mr Phillipson published some experimental pat-

12 Berlin work pattern. Five designs for slippers, c 1866

terns which met with little encouragement. Five years later Frau Wittich of Berlin, 'a lady of great taste' and an accomplished needlewoman, feeling that this 'species of amusement for ladies should be perfected' persuaded her printer husband to produce some more patterns. These turned out to be far more 'tasteful'. With this success and the coincidental invention of machine-made double-thread canvas, which greatly facilitated the operation, plus the newer, softer wools, Berlin work did not look back until it went out of high fashion in the 1870s.

Miss Lambert doubted that anyone ever equalled these early patterns by way of design or colouring. She was at pains to explain that the patterns were designed by artists paid 'in proportion to their talents'. Indeed they deserved to be. Less fair was the amount paid to those who did the actual colouring. The patterns consisted of squares (equalling the printed canvas ones) which were printed from copper plates on to what was called 'point paper' and coloured by hand by a process which even the apparently knowledgeable Miss Lambert confessed to finding 'curious'. Teams of men, women and children worked from complicated numbered charts, transferring the colours square by square. Even an industrious man could earn only 3s a day and a child as little as 6d to 8d. As some of the earliest designs (usually copies of paintings) cost the customer the staggering sum of £30 to £40 each, someone was making a nice profit. As copying was so much a feature of Berlin work it is hard to credit that Mrs Owen should feel that its great recommendation was that it encouraged *inventive* powers to a 'measureless extent'.

In England after the 1830s shops called Repositories soon sprang

up, especially in Regent Street in London where the most important was Wilke's Warehouse. This firm employed as many as 1,200
girls to colour the patterns. Not only did the original patterns
come from Germany but so did the wool. Called Zephyr (a mixture of Gotha and Spanish merino) it was much softer and easier to
work than the older, harder worsted. This softness made it possible
to use the new aniline dyes which were noted for their harsh bril-
liance and rich sombreness: crimson, magenta, veridian and Prus-
sian blue being the favourites. In 1812, during the Napoleonic
Wars, the importation of such wool was only 281 lbs but by 1833 it
rose to 25½ million lbs.

In 1840, the Countess of Wilton, author of *Art of Needlework*,
claimed that there were at least 10,000 Berlin patterns to choose
from; in 1847 Mrs Owen made it 14,000! She admitted that only
half (which must have been a generous estimate) were moderately
good and that the best were copied from English and French
prints. Mrs Owen was not happy about the colours. She thought
that pictures should resemble Gobelin tapestries: 'subdued and
beautiful'. She took the Berlin publishers to task for introducing a
bright blue sky into 'Bolton Abbey' which, she said, quite destroyed the 'stillness necessary to the inner court of a monastery'.
Another favourite was 'The Servant' taken from an 'interesting
relic of antiquity' which hung in Winchester College. It represents
a man and (oddly) a pig. The contemporary detailed instructions
sum up the striving for realism and the crude colours which so
characterise Berlin work. The pattern was obtainable from W.
Savage's 'China and Glass Warehouse, and Fancy Needlework,
Knitting and Crochet Repository' in Winchester. It dates from the
late '40s and shows that patterns had been, by then, necessarily
greatly reduced in price, since it cost only 2s 6d post free.

Although there was a quantity of complicated stitches (to be
found mainly on samplers, so one doubts that many of them were
actually used), the main stitches were tent (which could be worked
by 'the fingers of the little child to the trembling fingers of declin-
ing age'), cross or Gobelin. For such objects as birds, flowers and
fruit, a plush-like stitch was used. For this, loops were left standing
then cut and 'shaved' to give gradations of pile. For those ladies
who did not feel up to this task it could be given to a professional.
The Englishwomen's Domestic Magazine of 1863 informed its readers
that Mrs Wilcockson of 44 Goodge Street would cut and finish
such work for 2s 6d a canvas.

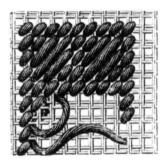

13 Three Berlin work stitches

The most popular canvas was 'Penelope', which had four warp
and weft threads woven together; 'German' had every tenth
thread dyed yellow to aid counting but was a rather cheap cotton
canvas. 'Berlin' was considered the best as it was made of fine black

14 Bead-work articles: a smoking cap of velvet; a velvet tea-cosy; a silk sachet; a 'miser' purse in knitted silk and steel beads; a wall-pocket; an evening bag. From 1840–1860

or white silk. 'Java' canvas was quite closely woven and good for large objects such as hearth rugs and carpets. It was still much used in the 1880s for everything from table cloths to travelling bags. One often sees a piece of Berlin work where the design is apparently not worked on canvas but on such material as fine linen or silk. This effect was achieved by tacking canvas to the material, stitching through both surfaces and when complete, removing the canvas threads. This was done for non-wearing objects such as fire-screens but for chair seats or footstools the threads were left in for strength. For the same reason the older, harder worsteds were often used for these items instead of the softer Zephyr wool.

Even at the beginning, Berlin work was not without its critics. As early as 1843 it was considered unsuitable for ecclesiastical purposes as being too 'foreign' for English churches! But in 1851 there was more serious criticism. Mrs Merrifield was shocked by the shameless copying of paintings, calling them 'those libels [and] . . . caricatures of human nature'. Perhaps she had just seen the six versions of Leonardo da Vinci's 'Last Supper' which were on show at the Crystal Palace. (One of these is at the Bethnal Green Museum, in London.) In 1908 Emily Leigh Lowes looked back on these pictures and called them 'wickedly hideous' and their colours 'vilely crude'. Although unfashionable by the '80s, Caulfield's *Dictionary* devoted some space to the subject even though it referred to the earlier 'impossible parrots, animals and groups of flowers [which had] done so much to debase the public taste as far as fancy work [was] concerned'. With rather too much trust in human nature the authors maintained that during the last few years the public had been taught to distinguish and appreciate the good from the false designs. With equal optimism they hoped that Berlin work would again take its 'ancient' (*sic*) position among needlework techniques. The *Dictionary* listed such stitches as 'Black', 'Damask', 'German', 'Herringbone', 'Irish' and 'Leviathan' (so called because it could be worked very quickly), 'Raised' and 'Repp', used singly, or even all at once on one piece.

Beadwork

When a Victorian lady carefully selected a coloured bead from either a partitioned box, a labelled bag or the lid of one of the boxes in which she had bought her beads, she could have had little, and most probably no, idea that she was, according to John Ruskin, encouraging the slave trade (Plates 14 and 43).

Beads only bore out Ruskin's assertion that one should never encourage the manufacture of anything unnecessary. He considered beads to be particularly so, as there was no design or thought in their manufacture. They were formed by the drawing out of glass

rods which, after various processes, were chopped up into different sizes and rounded off in a furnace. The worst part of the operation was that the ill paid 'slaves' who worked all day making
these beads, suffered from a vibration of the hands which resembled 'a perpetual and exquisitely timed palsy'.

Indicative of the public's ignorance (or indifference) is the fact
that Miss Lambert in 1843 described the whole process without so
much as mentioning the effect it had on the workers.

As a means of ornamentation beads go back to ancient Egypt.
When used during the Berlin work era the technique was often referred to as 'German Embroidery', patterns for which could be
bought from Berlin work Repositories. For all that she described
the making of beads Miss Lambert had a poor opinion of them,
considering them suitable for only small objects owing, as she put
it, to the 'paucity of colours'. But judging by existing examples the
range of colours seems to have been almost as wide as that obtainable in wools.

Opaque turquoise beads were recommended for background
work, better still if mixed with 'opals'. As well as glass, beads were
made of gold, silver, coral or garnet but, as Miss Lambert sternly
admonished, in the 'higher departments of art, when we wish to
imitate paintings' any sort of bead was 'totally inadmissible',
especially for historical subjects. The Germans, however, had no
such scruples and would have received a sharp rap over the
knuckles from Miss Lambert who called this country's use of beads
a 'gross infringement of all the proprieties of art' which all 'tasteful' Englishwomen could not 'too scrupulously avoid'.

In the 1840s the best beads were thought to come from Venice
but later those from France were considered to be far superior. It
was not long, however, before Birmingham and Stourbridge
manufacturers were flooding the British market with rather less
good versions. Steel beads (which had been very popular in the
eighteenth century) were used to outline flowers and leaves. As
steel was subject to rust it often quickly ruined many a carefully
worked piece. As well as the round beads one could buy long
bugles (used principally for fringes) and pearly ones for naturalistic 'highlighting'. Beads were often sold by weight when they
were known as 'pound' beads. There was a kind of beadwork for
flower motifs called *grisaille* which used a combination of white,
crystal, grey and black beads.

Beads came in various sizes. The largest (most suitable for children or those with poor sight) were comparatively easy to fasten but
the smallest presented a problem. Contemporary opinions differed
as to the correct method of sewing these. Even then, no needle was
fine enough to go through smaller beads, so that waxed thread was

advised. Once threaded on this the beads were transferred to a needle and sewn on separately; this was considered the 'best way'. An 'idle' one was to use the thread and to couch it down in rows but this had the disadvantage of being less secure. For making wholly beaded accessories such as necklaces, cuffs and bags a small tableloom was often used.

By the 1860s beadwork was out of fashion but Caulfield's *Dictionary* (often so much more in touch with what was really being made than what was in fashion) devoted about a column to this subject in 1882. To the authors the great advantage of beads over other forms of embroidery was that it was lasting, being affected by neither heat nor damp (unless steel were used), would not fade and could easily be cleaned with a damp sponge. By this time beads were chiefly used for trimmings on net or velvet for clothes, as even the *Dictionary* admits that sewing beads thickly on to velvet was very laborious—an indication that the world was speeding up and that women were no longer prepared to spend (or waste) much time in adorning themselves, or anything else.

Crochet

It is surprising that *Punch* (founded in 1841), out of all the occupations open to leisured ladies at this time, should have singled out crochet for one of its famous attacks on human foibles (Plates 15, 16, 28, 45 and 58).

In 1850 one of a series called 'Lessons for Little Ladies'—which was culled in First Primer style—contained this passage: '. . . she would pass all her time read-ing no-vels and work-ing cro-chet . . . but would ne-glect her house-hold du-ties.' In 1852 an article, 'The Law of Crochet', was more explicitly amusing and critical. It was a direct dig at the fact that 'cro-chet' was taking a wife away from her 'du-ties'. The 'Law' is written in quasi-legal language and begins:

Parliament has at length been compelled to give its over-tardy attention to the question deeply affecting the domestic happiness of her majesty's subjects. We allude to the Crochet question. The miseries arising from the unsettled state of the law upon this subject have resulted in an agitation which has made itself constitutionally heard. Meetings have been held in all the smoking clubs, in the lobbies of Operas, in the apartments of bachelor friends (after supper) and in the various places of refuge to which sufferers have been driven by Crochet persecution . . .

Nine clauses are listed. Among them that no woman was to work at Crochet more than fourteen hours out of the twenty-four. If a calf's head were served up badly cooked, the lady was not to blame

15 A pattern from the 'Victoria Crochet Patterns' range, c 1850

it on the fact that she had been too busy with her 'Boar's Head'—a pun, because the most popular crochet cotton was so named. The husband was to be allowed to taunt his 'Crotchetty' wife in 'any gentle and humorous way'. These being only two of the punning jokes so dear to *Punch* and the British.

In fact, crochet was the poor man's lace—the most easily made of all the imitation laces. By 1838 it was occupying middle-class women. So acceptable had it become by 1847 that Mrs Warren dedicated her *Court Crochet Collar and Cuff* to Queen Victoria, 'the patroness of every useful and elegant art'. By the early 1850s (when it was given the somewhat erroneous name of 'Point Lace') it had risen to 'great favour . . . in the fashionable world' as well as being one of the 'best channels for developing female industry'. It was therefore one of the few needlecrafts thought suitable for a 'lady' *and* 'the lower orders'.

Crochet has a long history. The English word for it is derived from the French *croches* or *croc* and Old Danish *krooke* for hook. It was known in the sixteenth century when it was worked chiefly in convents. It suffered a long lapse but saw a revival in the nine-teenth century in convents as well as being 'elevated' to the higher rungs of society. Once the basic chain stitch had been mastered the many variations were easy enough to work. The more compli-

16 Three stages of making a scalloped crochet edging, 1889

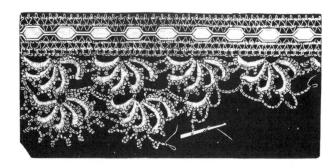

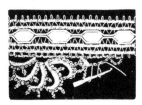

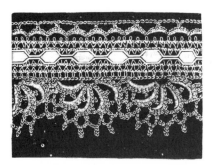

cated, such as 'Raised Rose' and 'Honiton', required a measure of skill but were chiefly worked for 'trade' purposes by 'the peasantry of England and Ireland'. The *Dictionary* listed over forty different stitches. Obviously for a 'lady' the simple chain, single, double, treble cross and treble were sufficient but by the '80s more stitches were thought fit for ladies to attempt as they were 'manifold in variety and as beautiful as they [were] numerous'. By combining many of them a 'tasteful and artistic bewilderment of threads could result'. 'Bewilderment', indeed, if not executed by very skilful hands; beautiful, if well done.

As well as Boar's Head and other cottons, Berlin wool, worsteds, nettings, silks, chenille, gold and silver cords and even fine braids—which must have been particularly difficult to work— were also used.

Knitting

From Shakespeare's 'knitters in the sun' to the *tricoteuses* at the foot of the guillotine and Queen Victoria knitting 'comforts' for her troops, this craft has been one of women's favourite occupations. It was particularly so during the nineteenth century when more articles than present-day scarves, jumpers, dresses, hats and baby clothes were knitted. Then they made knee preservers, flowered mats, bread-cloths and even curtains.

17 Knitting. Crossed casting on, forming a chain, 1886

Of older ancestry than crochet (the word is taken from the Saxon *Cnittan*) it was unknown in England until the sixteenth century when Queen Elizabeth I ensured its popularity by accepting a pair of knitted stockings as a New Year's present in 1560. But knitting was not fashionable until the early years of Victoria's reign when instructions began to appear in 'good' journals and books. Wool (called worsted) was the most common thread but cotton and silk were also much used, although the latter was not much advised.

Smocking

This is one of the oldest of crafts which for centuries was practised only by country people. Dating back to Anglo-Saxon times its various gathering stitches were a means by which some shape was given to a peasant's loose garment or smock. Embroidery was added to give further decoration and by the eighteenth century smocking had reached a degree of sophistication. The centre panel of the smock was pleated and joined by such comparatively simple stitches as 'chevron', 'rope' and 'basket' to the more complicated 'cart-wheel', 'whip-lash', 'waggoner' and 'reins and bits'—all redolent of country life. The plain side panels called 'boxes' were embroidered with motifs equally applicable to life in the country.

These included crooks, sheep-pens, hurdles and sheep. Milkmaids might sport butter pats and churns, and a gravedigger crosses and other symbols of death.

We are accustomed nowadays to many fashions moving from the 'lower orders' to the 'higher' but in the nineteenth century the reverse was the usual case. That is, except for smocking. In the late 1870s it was suddenly taken up by even high society and appeared on a variety of garments. In the 1880s it was much used by the 'arty' set headed by such people as Mrs Oscar Wilde who went in for anything 'simple' and 'countrified'. Weldon's published a series of booklets called *Practical Smocking* for those who wished to practise the craft at home. It was still fashionable in 1908 when *The Needlecraft Monthly* called it 'this delightful branch of needlecraft'; lamenting rather patronisingly that it had 'unfortunately died out as far as our peasantry are concerned'. They recommended it especially for children's dresses, for which it is still used today.

Netting

This work consists primarily of a succession of loops secured by knots. To keep the loops evenly spaced the work was done on a cushion or by fastening the foundation loop on one's foot with the help of a stirrup which, although an inelegant posture for a lady, was considered the best method. It could also be worked with a special ivory, bone or boxwood implement called a 'mesh'. (Plate 18) Many of the results look like ordinary fishnet but greater sophistication was achieved by elaborate darning.

Tatting

Of ancient lineage (the word comes from the homely old English *tatters*) this craft occupied many Victorian ladies from the middle of the nineteenth century and has recently seen a revival. An apparently fragile, rather haphazard-looking work, it is, in fact, much stronger than it looks. Unlike knitting and crochet where the stitches are interlocked, the stitches are joined by secure knots. At first only a needle was used but eventually shuttles were introduced. (Often the two were used together, which made the work much easier.) Like netting it consists of a series of loops and given scallops and medallions it was used for edgings and insertions.

Tambour work

Although of early Eastern origin, tambour work—so named because the frame resembles the French for drum and because it also looks like a tambourine—was unknown in Europe until the middle of the eighteenth century. Even then in Switzerland and Saxony it was only embroidered in white thread on cambric or

18 Netting. The Third Position of the Hands, 1886

muslin. In 1810 Maria Edgworth was surprised to receive 'a curiosity—a worked muslin cap that cost 6d done in tambour stitch' on 'a steam-engine'. She must have been referring to the machine-made net which was already in general production. Up to the 1820s this work was mostly done by the poor in Middlesex, Nottingham and in Ireland; only later was it taken up by 'the quality'.

The tambour frame itself consisted of two round wooden or iron hoops, the material being stretched tightly between them. The stitches, in a series of loops, were done with a needle rather like a crochet hook and it was a rather complicated operation (Plate 19). After practice it was possible to execute this stitch with some speed but by the 1880s when chain stitch became fashionable it was easier still. By then it was being worked on crêpe with gold thread in outline stitch filled in with coloured netting silk. Thicker materials such as cloth needed more care, when as well as the basic chain, *Point Lancé* (short straight lines), satin stitch and French knots were used.

19 Tambour work. Drawing out the thread with the special needle, 1886

Macramé

'Macramé lace! Macramé lace!' So began an 1883 advertisement for Barber's Thread, which called the craft 'the latest popular pastime and industry for ladies'.

Of Arabic origin (the word means fringe or trimming) Macramé was first mentioned in Italy in 1493 but was not much worked in England before the early 1880s. The technique consists of knotting threads to form a fringe and was also used for whole objects or as insertions. Silk was used for dresses and Maltese thread or twine for stronger items.

20 A macramé cushion. A fringe being worked, 1886

Some sort of cushion or frame was essential (Plate 20). Also needed were large-headed black pins and a crochet hook or fine knitting needle. A perfect result depended on the skill of the worker to space the pins evenly and to make each knot of equal tightness. It was first necessary to master the basic knots called 'bars', 'cords' or 'fillings'; from then on all sorts of patterns from 'Genoese Groppo' to 'Treble Stars' could be tackled. As well as the cushion a Tension Frame or Loom, known as 'Anyon's Patent', was invented in 1882 which consisted of a wooden frame fitted with levers and screws. This could be bought but could also be made at home. Instructions for making one were given in Butterick's *Needlework: Artistic and Practical* of 1889. It required a smoothly planed board, about 25 or 26 ins long and 12 or 14 ins deep (with nicely rounded edges) which had then to be covered on its upper side with several layers of flannel or cloth. Great care had to be taken not to wrinkle the material as this would impede the work. If the right sort of pins could not be obtained then small nails such as

43

21 Macramé. A typical tassel, 1901

carpet tacks or stout 'common' pins would do instead (Plate 21).

Quilting

'This term is employed to denote Runnings made in any material three-fold in thickness, i.e. the outer and right side of textiles, a soft one next under it, and a lining; the Runnings being made diagonal, so as to form a pattern of diamonds, squares or octagons, while serving to attach the three materials securely together.' A succinct description which comes from a nineteenth-century dictionary of needlework.

Quilting reached its peak of excellence in Europe during the eighteenth century when it was used principally for counterpanes and for petticoats when they were usually visible, but in England during the Victorian era it was chiefly used for bedspreads, the petticoat having become solely an undergarment. Different parts of the country produced their own distinctive designs. In the North traditional patterns such as 'feather', 'gable', 'fan' and 'star' designs persisted longer than in other districts. The most elaborate quilts were made in Allendale in Northumberland where they were called 'Gardiner' after a George Gardiner who hailed from this part of the country. He drew out the original pattern—often an elaborate floral one on a small diamond background—in blue pencil for which he charged between 1s 6d to 2s. Welsh quilts can be recognised by circular designs in the centre and corners while West Country ones, while also having circular motifs, have distinctive fan-shaped corners. A 'stripey' quilt consisted of rows or stripes in waves, shells, cords or tassels. To accentuate the striped effect strips of plain white material alternated with coloured ones and sometimes two differently printed cottons were placed side by side and quilted over.

Quilting was very much a cottage industry, not an occupation which many 'ladies' would take up. Even the menfolk in a poor family could be involved: making templates, threading needles and, if gifted, like Mr Gardiner, drawing the designs. A whole family could be working on one quilt at once but even professional workers could expect to get only about 5s a quilt—precious little for so much elaborate and exacting work.

At the poorest level quilts were filled with paper. Those philanthropic Victorians who encouraged the making of these salved their consciences by maintaining that being of a material 'very susceptible to atmospheric influences' they 'possessed warmth by retaining heat'. As many a down-and-out sleeping under his newspapers in the open could testify.

Patchwork

Primarily a way of using up odd scraps of material, patchwork was at first only made by the poor who could not afford a quilt or curtains in one material. During the eighteenth century patchwork began to reach middle-class homes, but even then only as part of a quilt; one finds few complete patchwork quilts in middle-class homes until about 1830.

The technique consists of cutting a number of various-shaped templates which are covered with material, sewn together, and the templates finally removed. Among the poor, all kinds of scraps were used—including remnants from tailors' and furnishing establishments who were only too glad to get rid of unsaleable goods. In the 1880s 1d bags of patches could be bought all ready for sewing. For those unable to afford even this, old pieces of blanket and shirts were put to use.

Ideally, patchwork is made of only one material such as cotton with cotton, silk with silk, and velvet with velvet. Silk could be combined with satin but care had to be taken if velvet were used with it. Needless to say, these latter materials were only for 'better class' work. For those who had, perforce, to mix a number of materials, it was advisable to wash them beforehand so that any shrinking or stretching was already done; otherwise, after washing the result could be a puckered disaster.

As with quilting, the men of the family were often involved in the stitching but principally in the cutting of the templates. These were made of many materials, from tin to paper. The best quality paper was considered to be directors' reports, although how the poor obtained such things is rather a mystery.

The shape of the template determined the pattern, and there were many patterns. The most usual and simple was the hexagon or honeycombe shape; then came diamonds, octagons, triangles (which made a box pattern), rectangles, loghouse (an American import), shell (which was complicated to join together), jewel, twist, right-angle—the list is almost endless. As an alternative to these regular designs it was also possible to make what was called 'crazy' or 'mosaic' patchwork which, as its names suggest, resembled crazy-paving paths. This form required no templates and was merely a matter of fitting together many different sized and shaped pieces, the joins being disguised with fancy stitches or couched cord.

Elizabeth Glaister, in her book *Needlework* published in 1880 was rather caustic about the whole subject of patchwork which by this time had already passed its peak of excellence. 'It is hardly too much to say,' she pontificated, 'that only here and there in the arrangement of a patchwork quilt did the worker herself

22 Patchwork: all silk in box pattern; part of a bedspread, c 1850

45

give any consideration to design, or to the due combination and balance of colour.' Although much patchwork *does* rely on these considerations, Miss Glaister seems to have missed the point that much of it achieves its effect by the fact that it is *not* constructed with much thought to balance (Plates 22, 33 and 78).

Appliqué

Appliqué means superimposing one material on another and is an old craft. The Victorians, however, could be rather vague about artistic periods. When in doubt about the date of anything they were liable to say that it was 'lost in antiquity' which, for them, gave it unquestionable worth. Appliqué does have some ancient names but the greatest source of inspiration for the Victorians was that executed during the Italian Renaissance (Plates 36 and 37).

During the eighteenth and early nineteenth centuries appliqué was done with restraint but the Victorians knew no such bounds. It is possible to impose practically any material upon another and given the challenge, the Victorians took it up with avidity. Velvet, plush, brocade, satin, cloth of gold or silver were overlaid with the same materials, and attached to the ground with stitching or couched down with cord and then often embroidered all over as

23 Appliqué. A seat or cushion cover, 1851

well. The lily was not only gilded—the poor thing was literally smothered. Velvet and plush were considered the only really 'good' foundations for gold, but velvet, plush, satin and silk were the most usual grounds. A rather more subtle variation was what was called *Broderie Perse* in which plain, self-coloured stuffs were mixed, the interest lying in the juxtaposition of various shades. Another technique was to cut flowers, leaves, birds, animals or figures out of cretonne and to assemble them into an ordered or 'scrap-book' effect.

Appliqué was even applied to such fragile materials as muslin and cambric, lace and net. Many examples are not true appliqué as they consist of different materials laid side by side. This was called 'Inlaid Appliqué' and was very much like 'crazy' patchwork, its joins being hidden by the same stitches. For big standing objects such as screens it was advisable to stick the pieces on to their ground before sewing. For those who could not be bothered to cut out and embroider the appliquéd shapes these could be bought already made, usually by machine.

Appliqué applies not only to cloth but also to feathers, animal skins, gold, silver, mother-of-pearl and what were called 'foreign substances'. Human figures were clothed in silk, velvet and jewels, animals in their appropriate skins and birds in their feathers. Such work resembles montage more than anything else; for an example of simpler, more acceptable, work of this kind see the felt seat cover in Plate 23.

Crewel work

In Mrs Oliphant's *Carita* published in 1877, the heroine is made to say: 'Let me get my work. It is a new kind of Art Needlework, Edward. It is a great deal better in design than the Berlin work we used to do, and it's in a very easy stitch, and goes quickly.' This was crewel work—as synonymous with Art Needlework as Berlin work had been with 'tapestry'.

This crewel stitch was only the old medieval stem stitch, newly named and given status by The Royal School of Art Needlework, the Aesthetic Movement and like-minded 'high art' practitioners and apologists. (Americans called it 'South Kensington stitch'.)

With the word 'crewel' however, we come to a muddle. Caulfield's and Seward's 1882 *Dictionary* put the problem very well. Under 'Crewel Stitch' it explains that this was 'one of the oldest embroidery stitches and well known in earlier times as Stem stitch; but since the revival of Crewel work, of which it is the most important stitch, its original name has become superseded by that of the embroidery associated with it'. To complicate the issue still further the actual wool was called 'crewel'. One could use crewel

wool without actually embroidering crewel work, just as one could use Berlin wool without engaging in Berlin work.

Under 'Crewel Work' the *Dictionary* rather dryly commented that it claimed 'to be raised from the level of ordinary fancy work'. Although Elizabeth Glaister in her *Needlework* of 1880 admitted that a great deal of what she so rightly called 'haze' still hung over the vexed question of Art Needlework she maintained that it was not merely an alternative to Berlin work but was a modern (*sic*) invention; the main point of it being that the embroideress must be creative, so that the piece of needlecraft could be lifted above the decorative into the realm of 'Art'. She agreed with many of her like-minded contemporaries that the work of the past must be seriously studied—so much for 'creativity'. She suggested going to heraldry, illuminated manuscripts, the rude scratches on a Moorish water jar, metal-work (particularly English and German) and Spanish braziers and bells which often had 'splendid' engraved borders. Aware of the dangers of such a doctrine, she disapproved of mere copying, arguing that the embroideress must not follow such examples in 'servile fashion' but 'glean' from the artists' work what would suit her needs.

But the power of design would not, she warned, come all at once. (In many cases, one fears, it never came at all.) She was even afraid that future generations would find such work too naturalistic and admitted that 'we have more science than culture; our technical skill is greater than our knowledge of art and we pay more regard to a lifelike representation of an object than to its proper decorative use'. Wise words. She went on to say that 'our protest is against the abuse of nature by servile and injudicious imitation from which needlework has suffered, in common with the nobler arts'. This thought is echoed even in the rather conservative pages of the Caulfield *Dictionary* of two years later which maintained that crewel work was difficult because it depended not so much on the skill of the actual stitchery or on the time and labour involved but upon 'the absolute necessity there is for the mind of the worker being more than a copying-machine, possessing the power of grasping and working out an idea on its own, and of being able to distinguish between a good or bad design or system of colouring'.

As to colours, those used in crewel work tended to be less strident than those of the good old Berlin work days. This was often because of a mistaken idea that 'old' work was muted and subtle; ignoring the fact that much of it only *looked* like this because it had faded. One has only to examine the unfaded interiors of seventeenth-century embroidered boxes to realise how bright the original colours really were. Miss Glaister was vaguely aware of this as she was critical of the unfashionable dowdy colours, saying these alone (especially if badly worked) did not *automatically* allow the work to pass 'under the sacred name of Art'.

This emphasis on 'creativity' was all very well for gifted ladies, but such words must have dismayed many untutored ones. How they must have longed for the days when all they had to do was to count the squares, without any obligation for executing a 'sacred work of art'.

But these ideals, however right or fine they were, were listened to, and practised, by only a few. To judge by the majority of patterns in journals and books of the '70s onwards the same old pas-

25 Crewel-stitch on linen, c 1893

49

tiche was very much alive from Surbiton to Edinburgh.

Transferring the Design An unannounced visitor entering a Victorian drawing room or parlour might well have been met with a curious if not a risible sight. He or she would have seen one of the ladies of the house leaning against a window pane and struggling with material, paper and pencil. She would not have been involved in some obscure rite but merely attempting to trace an embroidery design, this being only one of the many approved methods of carrying out this difficult job.

Up to the early years of the nineteenth century an embroideress or an artist would draw the outlines of the design free-hand on to the material—as many earlier unfinished pieces of work will testify. This method was always employed by the poor who could not afford anything else but the majority of Victorian ladies (even though they were usually taught to draw) cannot have been as expert or imaginative as their forebears if all the patterns and the instructions for transferring them which abound in this period are anything to go by. Berlin work with its squared patterns must have done a great deal to kill original drawing. An 'improved plan', which placed the outline on the canvas, was on show at the Great Exhibition but it was rarely used any more than the hot-iron transfer invented in 1874 for William Briggs (later to become the famous Penelope Company).

Many of these methods would, one feels, have taxed the skill and patience of a medieval craftsman, let alone an ignorant and helpless Victorian lady. Even in 1889 the best way of transferring a design was still by using parchment paper, which had the virtues of being transparent and strong enough not to tear in use. One had first to trace the outlines of the pattern on to the parchment with a pencil; then to take a tracing wheel (which made a series of little holes) and with it follow these outlines, taking great care when negotiating curves and corners. One then laid the paper on the rough side of the material and rubbed the perforated lines lightly with 'any good stamping powder', taking up enough of it (on a piece of chamois or flannel tied over a cork), to leave a clean impression. The next step was to remove the paper, lay a piece of tissue paper over the material and apply a warm iron to fix the dotted lines. If—and only if (as the instructions were so right to stress)—this had been *carefully* carried out, would the design be accurately transferred and the tissue paper could be removed. Even this was not foolproof as the result was liable to be indistinct. If this happened then the outlines had to be strengthened by Chinese White paint or white sewing cotton.

One could also use parchment and carbon paper. The latter was put under the former and the outlines traced with a metallic pencil or a knitting needle. One had to take care to prevent the whole thing slipping and not to press too hard.

'Rather more troublesome' (how could anything be?) than tracing, was old-fashioned 'pouncing'. This required as much patience as the other methods and more materials. Accustomed as we are today to being able to buy a bottle or packet of practically anything, it is hard for us to realise how many household things, from starch to glue, had to be made at home, especially if one lived in the country. The 'pounce' itself was the gum from the juniper tree reduced to a fine state—and this *could* be bought—but if unobtainable then finely powdered pipe clay darkened with a little charcoal was a possible alternative. The following is a *shortened* version of the rest of the process. After rubbing the real or simulated 'pounce' on to thick paper the design was then drawn on to it and the paper securely fastened to the cloth. The lines were then evenly pricked with a pin so that the pounce was transferred to the material. These dotted lines had then (as with the previous methods) to be 'fixed' with white paint. If the material were velvet or plush, or if it were very dark, then even more care and preparations were necessary. Pattern and material had to be secured with heavy weights and one had then to fill a small coarse muslin bag with white French chalk and run it through the pinholes. As the chalk was likely to blow away it had to be 'fixed' even more quickly.

Another ingredient which had to be made at home was the glue needed for certain kinds of appliqué. The ingredients were one teaspoon of essence of cloves and three and a half spoonsful of flour mixed with as much resin as would cover a halfpenny. This mixture had to be boiled and then turned out into a glazed earthenware pot to cool.

By the late '90s however, printed and transfer patterns were in much more general use and were often given away in journals or their cost was very little. Edwardian ladies did not have to cope with flying chalk or little concoctions cooling in earthenware jars.

5 By machine

'It would have been supposed that embroidery, the work of ladies' fingers, could never be supplanted by machinery, but such is the case.'

THE HAND-BOOK OF NEEDLEWORK Miss A. Lambert, 1843

26 A Swiss Jacquard loom weaving ribbons, which was shown at the International Exhibition of 1862

Many people imagine that Victorian needlework and lace was all done by hand. They ignore the fact that the Victorian age saw the flowering of one of the greatest periods of machine-invention the world has known. As Mary Simonds so aptly put it in her *Needlework through the Ages*, published in 1928, the nineteenth century went by to the 'accompaniment of the buzzing and whirring of machinery'. And this could not avoid being applied to all sorts of hitherto hand made needlecrafts. Most Victorians took pride in their ability to invent machines which, in a matter of hours, could turn out what had previously taken as many months to make by hand. But most had also scant regard for the fact that these machines put many people out of work and condemned the thousands who worked them to a life of drudgery and near-starvation.

When James Wyatt in 1733 spun the first thread of cotton on a model spinning machine, the die was cast and the clock, despite several desperate attempts to stop it, was never put back. Textile machinery went from strength to strength, pioneered by English inventors but soon aped by the French. The first lace-making machine was invented in 1798, followed by another in 1809 which could make bobbin net. The inventor was Joseph Jacquard who was asked by Napoleon if he were the man who 'pretends to do what the Almighty cannot do, to tie a knot in a stretched string?' Indeed he was, and there was no pretence. By 1837, three years after Jacquard's death, the Jacquard system with a loom named after him, was well established (Plate 26). Nottingham became the centre for machine made lace in England after the invention of the Hammond machine which produced a kind of knitted lace.

In 1777 net was made by the 'Pin' machine—so called because of the 'pins' which operated it. This machine continued its whirring way and even the Luddite Riots of 1811, when twenty-seven machines were destroyed, could not halt its progress. These nets were comparatively expensive but became cheaper after Heathcote (another inventor) lost his monopoly in 1823. Despite the fact that during the Napoleonic Wars the British Government forbade the export of any machines to France, tradition has it that one of Heathcote's employees smuggled a machine to Valenciennes in 1815. Soon bobbin-net machines in France were producing net, tulle and lace edgings. In Brussels, manufacturers specialised in embroidered machine-net of a high standard which at first was used only for bridal veils.

In 1820 'Grecian' net was made on a machine invented by a Nottingham manufacturer. It was a rather plain net but was soon supplanted by a spot pattern called *Point d'esprit* and other 'fancy' nets.

Machine embroidery was a different matter. But as early as 1775 C. F. Weisental took out a patent in England for an embroidery needle with an eye in the middle and a point at either end which could embroider muslin. In 1820, in England, a firm of cotton manufacturers in Mulhouse, run by Jose Heilman ran into financial difficulties. Necessity literally being the mother of invention caused Heilman to set about finding a remedy and he came up with an embroidery machine. As he wrote in his autobiography: 'The very words "machine embroidery" are never encountered in books on textiles—all the more reason for my endeavour.' By the end of 1828 he had made a machine 'of a most ingenious kind, which [enabled] a female to embroider any design with 80 or 140 needles as accurately and expeditiously as she formerly could with one'. This machine could do the work of fifteen hand-embroiderers and required merely the labour of one grown-up 'person' and two children under the supervision of a 'captain'. The main principle of this machine consisted of pincers which seized an equal number of needles and thrust them through the stuff at points to which they were guided by the operator, then released for other pincers to thrust them back again. The children's job was to thread the needles and to watch that no needle missed its appropriate pincer. A pantograph moved to and fro to trace the original design which was one-sixth of the size of the guiding pattern. This machine was used mainly for sprig patterns and dress material, borders for clothes, table cloths and valances.

In creating any pattern for a machine the designer needs to have a thorough understanding of how the machine works. Not only is this practical but also economical. In the early 1820s silk cost as much as 40s a pound, making any mistake expensive. Patterns were designed according to the amount the needle could take: thus two needlesful made one flower, three flowers one repeat, twenty repeats one border and four borders (rather obviously) made up a table cloth decoration.

This machine and some of its products were shown to the members of the Industrial Society of Mulhouse and won Heilman a medal. His machine also received a gold medal and its inventor the *Legion d'Honneur* when it had its first public showing at the Paris Exhibition of 1834 where it caused great interest. As a contemporary commentator put it: 'Whether at rest or in action, this machine was sure to be surrounded by a curious crowd. People never wearied of seeing in such a small space 130 embroidery needles, each one busily copying the same design and each one carrying out this task with perfect regularity.'

Despite the honours and the rather naïve interest, the French, surprisingly, did not take to this revolutionary machine, but more percipient firms in England and Switzerland were quick to see the possibilities. Mr Heilman sold the rights to Messrs Loechin (another Mulhouse textile manufacturer) who patented it in 1829. Then Mr Henry Houldsworth of Manchester, who owned a silk-weaving mill, took it over and improved it by doing away with the treadle and having the pincers operated by clockwork—thus putting even the children out of work. He went into business with Mr Louis Schwabe of Portland Street Mill when the machine was first put to commercial use. In 1845 Houldsworth took over the mill and until the end of the 1840s it was the only English embroidery machine in operation. But by 1859 there were twenty such machines at work and although other firms copied it, Houldsworth had the virtual monopoly until as late as 1875.

In 1843 Mr W. Cooke Taylor, author of *The Handbook of Silk, Cotton and Woollen Manufacturers,* visited the mill where he found the machine to be one of those 'most likely to engage the attention of the scientific visitor'. In 1844 Schwabe sent some samples of the machine's work to Queen Victoria, rashly claiming that it could execute any design her Majesty required. Taking him at his word, the Queen sent a drawing so complicated and large that poor Schwabe realised the folly of his boast. But as it was a Royal Command and his reputation was at stake, he resolved to carry out the design, cost what it would. The drawing was *so* big that a special card had to be prepared for the pantograph and only one needle could be used—so that it was a profitless venture. Unfortunately no record exists of this example of manufacturer's vanity and naïve royal faith. We do know that it was an elaborate floral design making great use of 'ombre' or shaded effects which, by this time, the machine was well able to achieve.

The earliest piece in existence from this machine is a simple floral design on Alpaca made in 1849. *The Journal of Design and Manufacturers* which promoted it, had no false modesty as to its virtues, calling it 'a very successful run for the spring trade'.

At the Great Exhibition, Houldsworth's machine attracted a good deal of notice, as did specimens of its work such as quilts and 'medallions', which were probably for use in appliqué. Many other firms showed similar machines and wares. Birken's displayed black silk flounces, falls (veils), trimming laces, etc; Adams & Sons showed laces and edgings; Heymann & Alexander displayed 'machine-wrought' cotton lace curtains as well as cotton extra twist Brussels net and Zephyr net for embroidery. Herbert & Co's contribution was lace and crochet lace made on a warp-and-twist machine. There were machine made ribbons, table cloths, shawls and handkerchiefs. Nottingham lace curtains 'made entirely on the lace Jacquard application' were much in evidence.

In 1859 George Wallis (who had worked for Houldsworth's firm from 1848 to 1849) delivered a lecture on machine-embroidery to the Royal Society of Art. In it he described how the machine worked and (with typical Victorian smugness) maintained that the monotonous grind involved was 'a branch of factory labour for females' which could be both 'healthful' and 'interesting'. One wonders how 'healthful and interesting' *he* would have found standing hour after hour feeding needles with endless yards of cotton.

Oddly enough he does admit—and in this we hear the Victorians justifying themselves—that this mechanical embroidery, far from interfering with hand-labour, did much to foster it. In London alone, 2,000 'persons' obtained their living by embroidery who had never done so before.

Soon other countries were cashing-in on the machine-embroidery boom. Even Switzerland which, from the end of the eighteenth century had been famed for its hand made muslin embroideries, imported a machine in 1829. It was modified in 1834 when six muslin-embroidering machines were in use. Even this work had to be finished off by hand and eyelet holes, or what we would call broderie anglaise, was still beyond the powers of a machine.

This particular technique was not mastered even by the 1850s when fashion dictated that no lady could be well dressed unless her collar, chemisette (a kind of dicky) and sleeves were not all in hand or machine embroidered muslin. It was not until 1869 that M. Oettle invented a machine which successfully embroidered eyelet holes; even so the holes had first to be cut by hand.

John Ruskin naturally raised a loud voice against the ever increasing influence of the machine, especially applied to needlework. Himself the instigator of hand made 'Greek' lace (see chapter four) he waxed indignantly (and poetically) on the subject. 'A spider,' he maintained, 'may perhaps be rationally proud of his own web, even though the fields in the morning are covered with the like, for he made it himself, but suppose a machine had spun it for him? Suppose all the gossamers were Nottingham made?' (One can't help feeling that the spider, assuming he could ever possess a 'rational' mind, would have been grateful to have the labour taken away from him.) Ruskin went on: 'If you think of it, the whole value of lace as a possession depends on the fact of its having BEAUTY which has been the reward of industry and attention'—missing the point that machine made lace was just as much the product of industry and attention as hand made, as well as being much cheaper, and not necessarily less BEAUTIFUL.

Even he, of course, could not stem the tide. By the 1870s, machine made trimmings of all sorts dominated the fashion scene, so much so, that contemporary writers thought that such trimmings would be the outstanding mark of the period.

In 1830 a machine was invented in Paris to make chain stitch, but like so many early machines it was destroyed by a fearing-to-be-put-out-of-work mob. Although further attempts were made in England in the 1840s it was not until 1856 that the rapidly emerging United States found in E. A. Gibbs an inventor who could perfect a single-thread chain-stitch machine; even so it was not until ten years later that a Frenchman took the idea far enough to make it a commercial proposition. It was the American Mr Singer who revolutionised home-dressmaking by inventing the sewing machine. Patented in 1849 it was shown at the Great Exhibition two years later. Even at the beginning it could manage simple embroidery stitches but it cannot have been very successful or much used because in 1878 it was admitted that 'We must wait for better results and for the moment leave the sewing machine to be used for purely utilitarian purposes.'

The largest expansion of machine embroidery was still in the British Isles. In 1870 the firm of Houldsworth had become Todd & Co but it was still the only really important firm. In 1875 however, Gibson, Brother & Co of Glasgow brought out fourteen machines which were used mainly for making mourning clothes. This was a big industry in the days of large families and a high death rate when people went into mourning for even the remotest cousin; indeed, it is hard to imagine that many people were ever out of mourning. Gibson's also made curtains, furnishing fabrics, white embroidered muslins and tulles. For the sake of economy the muslin was bleached before it was machine-embroidered with cotton. This meant that the workers had to wear special white overalls and canvas overshoes and wash their hands before being allowed near the machines—which were more valuable than people.

As the century progressed more and more machine-laces became available. In the '80s there was 'burnt out' lace. By a complicated process the background was dissolved, leaving the 'lace' in one piece. It is one of the most realistic of machine made laces and is often hard to distinguish from the real thing. In the '90s and early 1900s when lace was so fashionable, for blouses in particular, those ladies 'unprovided with [a] liberal dress allowance' could use machine made lace as it was so much cheaper than real lace.

The fault of much nineteenth-century English machine made lace or embroidery was that manufacturers tried to achieve too regular a result; the French were better at achieving the irregularity which gave the machine variety more of a hand made look. But in 1900 *The Art Journal* claimed that England led the world in 'natural looking' machine made lace and other fabrics.

The first Scottish machine made lace was made in 1874 on Derval looms set up by Messrs Morton & Co in the valley of Irvine and the results were said to rival those of Nottingham. The first Morton designs were inspired by Italian Renaissance, Tudor and Early English styles but by the '80s and '90s, in line with changed taste, more designs were taken from French, Moorish and Japanese sources. The treatment was on the whole realistic: flowers and fruit motifs in particular having 'a certain freedom and decorative grace'. The firm was able to employ many well-known artists such as Charles Voysey, one of the important names in the Art Nouveau Movement. Not having William Morris's objection to the machine he designed for woven fabrics and also for muslin curtains, as did another Art Nouveau artist, Lewis F. Day, who had founded the Art Workers' Guild in 1884. By 1900 this firm's lace curtains had become more complex and 'in a sense, more lace-like'. That taste had changed is evident from the fact that the firm did not claim to rival the 'real thing' as this was not only impossible but undesirable—a strong contrast to the earlier Victorians' delight in making one material look like another (Plates 27 and 73).

Ruskin and Morris were not the only ones to criticise the machine. The author of *Embroidery and Lace* published in 1888 asked, 'Are mechanical processes ceaselessly pouring forth abundant quantities of things, to supplement artistic handicrafts?' With 'lace' curtains being woven at the rate of 700 yards a day at one factory alone in 1900, it seems that they could.

27 Machine lace curtains with an embroidered lambrequin or pelmet with matching tie-backs, 1876

6 In the home

'It must be borne in mind that each object in the room that is ornamented with a pattern requires, and even insists upon, an effort of mind for its comprehension, and many people find it impossible to pass over anything.'

NEEDLEWORK   Elizabeth Glaister, 1880

At no other time in history have houses been so over crowded and over decorated as they were between about 1830 and 1914.

By 1837 some rooms still retained a certain eighteenth-century and Regency simplicity. This can be seen in many paintings of this time when one piece of furniture can be distinguished from another—often a difficult task when looking at paintings or photographs of rooms in the 1890s.

Much of this can be put down to the new attitude towards interior decoration which began in about the 1830s. In the eighteenth century when rooms had less furniture in them a unity of style and colour was the aim. This was seen at its richest and best in the work of the Adam brothers but was also to be found in less grand homes where a whole family and even the servants would embroider a matching set of chair and sofa covers. By the 1840s, however, when taste was much more eclectic, it was thought quite correct to have as many diverse patterns, fabrics and designs as possible.

There were some exceptions, of course, such as William Morris's Red House, decorated completely in 'Medieval' style, and many interiors of the 1870s and '80s which were under the influence of the Aesthetic Movement. Those who followed the precepts of Art Nouveau artists, designers and architects, revived an eighteenth-century unity but for the majority, cheerful or sombre clutter was the order of the day.

In a typical Victorian or Edwardian interior needlecraft of every description played a large and important part. Even so it was up against heavy competition. As Elizabeth Glaister put it in 1880: 'Wallpapers, carpets, painting, carving, inlaying, metal work— some of these, if not all, will contribute divers forms and colours or ornament to the room before the women are invited to take up the needle.' Mrs Orrinsmith in 1878 had been far more caustic and critical when she described a typical drawing room which contained such things as:

coal-scuttles ornamented with highly coloured views, of say, Warwick Castle; *papier maché* chairs inlaid or painted with natural flowers or pictures; hearthrugs with dogs after Landseer in their *proper* colours; mats and footstools or foxes startlingly life-like with glaring glass eyes; ground glass vases of evil forms and sickly pale green or blue colour; screens graced by a representation of 'Melrose Abbey by moonlight' with a mother-o'-pearl moon. Carpets riotous with bunches of realistic flowers, chintzes with bouncing bouquets, chairs with circular seats divided into quarters, of black and orange, their backs composed of rollers of the same alternate stripes; chiffoniers, with mirror-doors too low for any purpose save to reflect the carpet in violent perspective, or perchance a novel view of a visitor's boots.

It is as if middle-class Victorians and Edwardians needed to surround themselves with as many elaborate and heavy or even fragile possessions as possible in order to shield themselves from the stark realities of the outside world.

So many objects and accessories could be made entirely of or decorated with needlecraft that it is almost impossible to assign them to a particular room: the same curtains, chairs and pictures, for instance, could be found in the parlour or in the bedroom. It is better, therefore, to deal with categories one by one, occasionally assigning such an object as a bed or dining cloth to its appropriate room.

Curtains

'Any lady who is clever with her fingers can make handsome window curtains'—so wrote the anonymous author of *Needlecraft: Artistic and Practical* in 1889. R. H. Haweiss in 1888 referred to windows as 'transparent walls', which indeed they often were, but during the nineteenth century such was the tendency to cover them up with draperies, this was often not apparent. So adverse were some people to looking out of a window that ladies even occupied their time painting the panes in imitation of stained glass.

As well as the heavy main curtains there was a great vogue for centre or inner curtains made of flimsier material. In the 1840s such curtains were often made of darned net and even knitted in a light feather pattern. Crochet was popular for whole curtains, and as borders or insertions (Plates 28 and 29).

28 The bottom of a linen curtain with crochet insertions and border, cut-work and drawn-thread work, c 1890

The main curtains of 'gaudy velvets, crackling silk, stiff damasks and harsh rep' were made even more fussy with lace or muslin loops, cords and tassels. It was not until the late 1870s, with the advent of Art Needlework, that curtains were considered suitable objects for embroidery or appliqué. Mrs Orrinsmith advocated 'richly dight or fair embroidered [curtains] hanging in noble folds'. For winter, velvet, serge, cloth or Bolton sheeting could be embroidered with outline patterns in long chain stitch in various hues, shading from deep red to pale yellow to give a 'delightfully calm, warm and rich' effect. For a softer one then 'quiet' green material embroidered with dull gold and shaded with a few touches of deep orange would prove very satisfactory.

Light-weight curtains were hung for summer. But Mrs Haweiss was not in favour of white as, she maintained, it kept out neither heat nor light. Instead, she suggested the use of 'delicately hued' and patterned Madras muslin or Indian Tussore silk which was, in fact, a dress material. These fabrics could be embroidered with silk or crewels but if a number of colours were used then it was advisable to give such curtains a border of white or yellow to 'conduce an even surface of tone'. Instead of stiff roller blinds, Mrs Haweiss was in favour of half-curtains (or café-curtains as the Americans now call them) made of muslin, Tussore or fine Holland and given an embroidered border. Rep was considered too stiff to hang well and woollen damask was not recommended; the best materials were cloth, serge (or 'diagonal' as it was often called), velvet or heavy satin as these 'true and well-woven' stuffs had the advantage of hanging well and being pleasant to work on—especially in the

29 Lawn inner curtain with a panel of darned net, surrounded by broderie anglaise. Edged with pillow-lace. Lawn pelmet with insertions and edging of pillow-lace and tassels, c 1880

hand as such large surfaces could not be put into a frame. Crewel wool could be used but silk was thought better; it was considered inadvisable to use appliqué on velvet as the pile was so thick. As an example of what was thought smart in the '80s one design consisted of red poppies worked in outline stitch on dark brown velvet.

Less exotic and less expensive materials were linen and Bolton sheeting which could be safely worked with either wools or silks. A branching pattern of large flowers and leaves was thought very good or one could cover a curtain with the heraldic device of 'powdering'; that is, scattering motifs at regular intervals.

A dado or deep border along the bottom of a curtain was much in fashion in the '80s and '90s especially if the room were very high. The design usually consisted of a row of flowers for which the 'middle tints' were thought best. In line with the still prevailing taste for Gothic, other heraldic devices could be used such as appliquéd birds and beasts in their 'proper' colours as well as texts formed of Medieval letters in appliquéd tape.

In about 1880 a novelty in the form of black lace (called 'Cabul') curtains came into vogue which obviously went well with a room already decorated with dark panels. At this time patterns for knitted curtains were still available along with those for borders in crochet, macramé and other techniques although these hand made curtains had strong competition from Nottingham machine made lace. Ecru and shades of cream and gold were available in lace and other light stuffs but nothing (despite what Mrs Orrinsmith said) could compete with white. As Emily Moberly, reminiscing about her childhood in 1852 remembered: 'I think one of the chief delights was the white dimity curtains in the bedrooms; they, in their freshness, always contained a good deal of the essence of the first evening in the country, when we children roamed from room to room . . .'

Portieres

'As a rule, one side of a door should be protected by a curtain for the prevention of those icy draughts which every thoughtful builder constructs for the benefit of his brother the undertaker.' So, dryly, Mrs Haweiss in 1881.

These door-curtains, often called *portieres,* are a great feature of most nineteenth- and early twentieth-century homes. Before our age of smaller rooms, better fitting windows and central heating they must have been a necessity (Plate 30).

As well as every door being given its *portiere* in a large home, gaps were made in walls to create vistas from room to room. During the summer these openings admitted 'sunny rays and cool breezes' when the *portiere* would be caught back but in winter it had to look well on both sides. For the 'important' side (that is, the one in the larger room) it was suggested that a scarlet curtain be appliquéd in black velvet bands embroidered in gold, while the other or 'less important' smaller-room side, was given a pattern in black outline embroidery. For a curtain over a door the treatment could be simpler but for both openings horizontal designs were to be preferred to vertical. In the '80s, as with window curtains, a branching pattern could be used instead. 'Dark blue' runs an instruction at this period, 'may have a pattern of oranges, leaves and flowers worked in crewels.' The writer advised using only six colours as 'a whole shopful of varied hues will not produce so good a decorative effect'. By the '90s it was considered more important that the *portieres* should harmonise as much as possible with the rest of the room—that is, in 'modern' homes; others were often just as much a jumble of colours as ever.

Not only were doors and gaps given curtains but so were bookcases (Plate 31), cabinets and pictures 'perhaps too sacred to expose to the general eye'. If the frame were gilt then crimson silk embroidered with gold was thought appropriate; if walnut or ebony then the curtain should be white and silver.

Most of these curtains needed tying back. If this were not done with heavy tasselled cords, metal curtain-bands or ribbon, then the artistically minded could make them by hand. Berlin work was popular; so were scarves. If made out of pongee or India silk a scarf could be embroidered with metallic cord or even lustre painted. Black velvet was considered especially good as it took metallic embroidery so well. Even common ticking, in the traditional colours of blue and white stripes, was used. But this was not, of course, left alone: the white stripes were embroidered in many colours and the blue almost covered in tinsel cord or braid. It was only by Edwardian times that people began to realise that unadorned ticking has a beauty of its own.

Pictures

The walls of most Victorian and Edwardian houses were covered in pictures, many of them in needlework. Some would be the elegant Regency hand painted and silk-embroidered ones in black and gold frames but many would more likely be silk or Berlin work copies of paintings.

One of the most celebrated of embroiderers of wool pictures was Miss Mary Linwood who was born in 1755 and died in 1845. She copied Old Masters in wools on canvas using long and short stitches which followed the form of the object or person. Examples can be seen at the Victoria and Albert Museum, London and at the Queen's House at Kew. Miss A. Lambert, writing in 1843, made

30 *Portiere* which could be made of plush, raw silk, satin or cretonne, given appliqué flowers and tied back with tasselled cords, 1889

31 *Portiere* for a bookcase, made of silk, ornamented with embroidered velvet, edged with cord and given a Turkish fringe, 1889

32 Berlin wool picture. 'The
Talisman' from Walter Scott's
novel, c 1860

the extraordinary claim that it was 'scarcely to be imagined that
any needlework, either in ancient or modern times, has ever sur-
passed Miss Linwood's celebrated productions'. Anticipating William Morris, Miss Linwood had her material, a kind of tammy
(which is a combination of cotton and worsted), and her wools
dyed to her specifications. She began her life-long work when
only thirteen and soon became famous. She held her first exhibition when she was thirty-two in 1789, and in 1798 opened a
'Gallery of Pictures in Worsted' in Leicester Square, which was to
become one of the sights of London. She copied many paintings by
(for her) such contemporary artists as Reynolds, Stubb and
Gainsborough as well as the Old Masters. She refused the then
staggering sum of three thousand pounds for her copy of Carlo
Dolci's 'Salvator Mundi' (which was considered her best piece)
and bequeathed it to Queen Victoria. In 1843 her collection numbered sixty-four pieces, including a self-portrait. But she outlived
her fame, and by her death in 1845 other techniques had made her
old-fashioned so that her whole collection fetched only about
£1,000.

For all that, she must have been the inspiration for the flood of

Berlin work pictures which had begun before her death. Religious subjects were very popular, especially Leonardo's 'Last Supper' and Raphael's 'Transfiguration', 'Christ and the Woman at the Well' and 'Joseph Presenting his Father to Pharaoh'—this last often embellished with jewels, pearls and sequins. Moses could be discovered in woolly rushes by a singularly Turkish-looking Pharaoh's daughter: the Victorians were never very good at historical accuracy. Competing with the religious theme was a wave of Romanticism which swept the country from the 1830s onwards, inspired by Walter Scott's novels and the Gothic revival. The Stuarts were very popular. In tent or cross stitch Mary Queen of Scots 'mourned the death of Douglas at the battle of Langside' or 'bade farewell to her Ladies before her execution'. Also popular were scenes from the Civil War when the Cavaliers (so much more romantic than the Roundheads) were usually shown in a favourable light. Sentimental animal pictures were also all the rage and here Landseer could supply his 'Stag at Bay'. His topographical pictures such as 'Bolton Abbey in the Olden Time' and 'Chevy Chase' were often much copied as were George Moreland's bucolic scenes. Engravings and other prints were used and such sources as *Drawing Room* books and *Keepsakes* as well as bird, animal and floral tomes were ransacked for ideas.

A new subject was contemporary royalty. Few people had chosen to embroider the unpopular Hanoverians but a new young queen (even though she was a Hanoverian herself) was a different matter. For one thing she had a handsome husband, and for another a large family; her blameless family life was much respected and emulated by the Victorians. The Queen was shown with her children or the children were embroidered on their own. Edward, the Prince of Wales—in sailor's uniform, or in Highland dress perched precariously on a branch or with one foot on a dog—was particularly popular.

Footstools

As well as seeing him on the wall (or on a firescreen) one could also tread the infant heir to the throne underfoot as these designs were also used on many a footstool. This fact worried Mrs Merrifield in 1846. She thought that stepping on the sacred person of a royal child was a form of *laise majesté*. As well as royalty, children and pets were favourite subjects for footstools.

The negotiating of a typically overcrowded Victorian or Edwardian drawing room or parlour must have been a perilous undertaking. Not only would it be filled with furniture and objects but also with a multitude of footstools, often of different sizes and heights. These must have proved a veritable obstacle race

33 Stool with patchwork cover. Diamonds and hexagons, making a star pattern, edged with cord and thick fringe, 1882

for crinolined or bustled ladies, boisterous children, pets and any gentleman foolish enough not to look where he was going—let alone servants carrying trays. An alternative to the footstool was the hassock which (opposed to the footstool which was mounted on wooden feet) was made entirely of material and was a good object for embroidery as was the even larger and heavier Otto-man.

Chairs

From these objects it is a small move to the chair. By the 1830s the elegant Regency drawing room or dining room chair had become heavier, more bulbous and more carved. Its back and seat were good surfaces for ladies wishing to try out their Berlin work. Most of the designs were floral (Plates 34 and 35); Gothic patterns were used on those low-seated, high-backed chairs called *Prie-dieu* which were used for private or public prayers. High-backed Queen Anne style chairs of the 1850s were also given Berlin work coverings. Mahogany or walnut stools with 'X' shaped legs were also covered in wool work where the design was more likely to be geometrical than floral.

In the 1880s heavy 'Elizabethan' or 'Cromwellian' chairs were popular, given embroidered or closely-laid braid seats and fringes. Also in the '80s deck-chair like seats were fashionable covered in either thin carpet or embroidered canvas (Plate 36). By the '90s more delicate cane chairs were coming in, their seats often embroidered to resemble brocade. By the 1900s if a chair were given an embroidered seat at all it was carried out in the fashionable 'Louis VI' style, or if one were Art Nouveau minded, one embroidered a pink rose on pale green linen.

Cushions

When Berlin work was at its height the majority of cushions were covered in a variety of flowered patterns from an all-over design to a spray on a plain ground (Plate 38). Stripes were also popular as well as a wavy 'Florentine' pattern (Plate 39) which must have been as trying to the eyes to work as it is to look at. For such patterns a typical colour scheme would be yellow, blue, scarlet, green and lilac, relieved with black and white. Shading was very à la mode, each colour being worked from the middle of the design, shading to light or dark on either side.

Even black lace was imitated in Berlin work and much used on cushions. Using an open net ground the 'lace' design was worked in fine black silk, the finer and closer parts being overlaid with thicker silk in cross stitch.

By 1870 Berlin work cushions were on the wane. Instead of their

34 Mahogany drawing-room or bedroom chair. Covered in Berlin wool work the design echoes the florid carving of the frame, c 1855

'gaudy obtrusiveness' crewel work was much more likely to be found, worked in subtle colours on linen or any other 'natural' material. In the '80s bolster or sofa cushions were fashionable (Plate 40). Made of rep, silk, velvet or cloth they were often trimmed with lace bows and cords. For the ultimate in the exotic a piece of brocade was even embroidered and ornamented with couched cord.

There was also the shoulder cushion which would be made of Java canvas cut on the cross. As in drawn-work, threads would be

35 Back and seat for a similar chair.
Worked but not made up. Berlin
work in wool and silk, c 1860

36 Folding or 'American' chair. Covered in serge with a band of embroidered appliqué edged with cord, 1878

37 Detail of the folding chair

38 Silk boudoir cushion embroidered with silks in crewel work, c 1875

39 Berlin work cushion cover,
worked but not made up.
Florentine stitch in wool and silk,
c 1850

40 Two sofa pillows: (*top right*)
plush and satin, edged with cord and
embroidered in stem stitch with a
rosette of ribbons; (*right*) satin and
velvet, edged with cord and
embroidered in stem stitch. Such
cushions were often perfumed, 1889

taken out, the ones left being plaited and worked over in cross
stitch. There were patchwork cushions (each patch being outlined
in cord) and many 'point' stitches from *Guipure d'Art* to *Point de
Venice* were mounted on velvet or plush. Pretty boudoir cushions
would consist of a circle of cloth embroidered and bordered with
ruched satin and Guipure lace.

Anti-Macassars

'Under the Immediate Patronage of the Courts of Europe, the

41 Art Nouveau-inspired cushion, decorated with cut-work and running stitches, c 1900

42 Linen cushion in cut-work, Venice and tulle point, 1908

Aristocracy, and the Upper Classes. Rowland's Macassar Oil. Is universally in high repute for its remarkable virtues in *nourishing, improving* and *beautifying* the HUMAN HAIR.' So ran an 1851 advertisement. Despite such patronage and such virtues this oil had the great disadvantage of soiling any material with which it came into contact, especially the backs of chairs or sofas. Hence the need, during most of the nineteenth century and later, for what was called an anti-macassar—though it was known by other names during its history. As Mrs Warren in her *The Court Crochet, Collar and Cuff Book* (which did not confine itself to these subjects) of 1847 put it: '. . . as long as hair requires oil or pomade, so long will these useful decorations be needed.' According to her a house without an anti-macassar showed a 'poverty of industry'.

Anti-macassars could be netted, knitted or made of crochet. A pink crochet one strung with purple beads sounds nauseating but even worse must have been a design called 'Kaleidoscope' which combined crochet with strips of braid-work and tatting. Many anti-macassars were made of Berlin work in wool or beads (Plate 43). As well as the usual oblong, one could make this object in the

43 Anti-macassar. Berlin bead work. Lilies, coral and 'Gothic' border, c 1860

shape of a bag or envelope which fitted snugly over the back of a chair or sofa. As it could not slip out of place it was considered a great improvement when it was introduced in the 1850s.

In the '60s another name was coined for this ubiquitous item: the French *housse*. Lady Alford refers to it in her *Needlework as Art* in preference to anti-macassar which she considered horrid. Not that she was in favour of the thing, whatever it was called, considering it a 'petty disfigurement'. She thought that crochet was particularly unsuitable as 'well-regulated' eyes would suffer from the glaring white of such work; ignoring the fact that much crochet was carried out in colours. 'Chair-backs' as she *really* preferred to call them should, she felt, be sparingly used and 'artistically disposed'.

By the '80s the word 'tidy' was substituted, by which time it was being made out of embroidered silk or serge and cannot have been easy to keep clean. Which is perhaps why Elizabeth Glaister in 1880 suggested that linen or ecru silk only 'slightly' embroidered or decorated with drawn-work, would be better. Most homes must have had far too many of them for she tartly commented that 'if we must have tidies, let them be put where they are really wanted'.

But like so many reformers, Lady Alford and Miss Glaister spoke largely in vain for the tidy, or whatever you chose to call it, became, if anything, even more elaborate and unwashable. One of the most complicated was made of scrim threaded with ribbon for which even a special needle was required. A particularly fancy and highly insanitary tidy was made out of panels of plush, velvet, silk and satin bordered with lace which could be 'expensive or not, as desired'.

By Edwardian times chair or sofa backs (by this time sometimes called 'veils') were usually made of broderie anglaise or Richelieu work on linen, edged with lace.

Table cloths

With so many tables of all shapes and sizes cluttering up practically every room and even landings and corridors it is not surprising that they should be covered in cloths—or 'covers' as they were more usually called.

In the early years Berlin work was much used for cloths when they were given fringes of lace, crochet, tatting, macramé or chenille. The latter, in 1843, was considered (apart from gold and silver) to be the most expensive of embroidery threads. It took its French name from its close resemblance to a species of caterpillar and was much used to embroider table covers in patterns of flowers, birds and arabesques. *Chenille à broder* was the finest (in silk or wool) and that called *Ordinaire*, as its name suggests, the coarsest and used chiefly on canvas and even for crochet work.

During the '50s cloths were also made of beadwork, patchwork and covered in braiding. Many of these cloths were decorated only around the border—the deeper the better. Such a one was exhibited at the Great Exhibition with a series of appliquéd Renaissance cartouches worked in gold thread on moreen, which was either a coarse or silk damask-like tammy. This exhibition also showed cloths which were more remarkable for their size than any artistic merit. Mrs Penley of Margate (designer and manufacturer) showed a silk patchwork cover in box pattern which consisted of nearly 2,000 pieces needing 500,000 stitches. Mr Johnson of Airdrie in Scotland spent 18 years of his leisure-time making a table cover composed of 2,000 pieces of cloth. Another cover used as many as 2,000 pieces of broad-cloth.

In the late '70s, under the influence of Art Needlework, cloths were more often made of crewel-embroidered serge. Fine Java canvas was also popular as was embroidered *satin de chine*. Walter Crane designed two table covers for the Royal School of Art Needlework; one with cowslips, the other daffodils and butterflies—such country motifs having largely superseded the old exotic cabbage roses and lilies.

In 1880 Elizabeth Glaister had much to say on the subject of table covers. In her *Needlework* she wrote: 'If the tables in our rooms have been chosen according to the pretty specimens figured in the earlier volumes of this series [*Art at Home*] they will not want any cloths.' But she had to admit that 'for comfort in use in wear, for whist, or the elder ladies' bezique a cloth is essential'. She did not recommend linen or flax because these would slip off the table; she suggested serge instead. Despite this she was no advocator of Art Needlework, claiming that many 'outrages' had been committed in its name. She considered white cloths in drawing rooms 'suggestive of crumbs and a promiscuous repast'. She liked rich as well as the simple embroidery techniques in the form of borders. She was not in favour of fitted cloths and felt that cords and fringes were not an improvement—Miss Glaister had a refreshingly uncharacteristic un-Victorian attitude to decoration.

Alas, it was not generally shared, for in the '80s and '90s many extremely complicated cloths were popular. Java canvas was appliquéd with dark blue velvet lozenges, surrounded by stars and circles of woollen cross stitch in three shades of crimson; black cloth was appliquéd with two shades of bronze; yellow cloth was fastened down with braids and overworked with various fancy stitches in gold and bronze silks—etcetera, etcetera.

Less exotic were coloured German linen cloths embroidered in

44 Damask breakfast cloth, with
drawn-work, satin-stitch
embroidery and thick fringe.
Matching serviettes, 1878

silks, but even these could be given complicated drawn-work borders. Despite the dictates of fashion, Berlin work borders were still
being made as well as those composed of intricately entwined
fancy braids.

The early 1900s saw a move towards simplicity. As well as the
odd Art Nouveau flower or peacock feather there was a taste for
Chinese-style cloths, and those worked in imitation of blue and
white Dutch Delft tiles. The 'peasant' look was also fashionable. A
technique called 'Hardanger' which came from Norway used
thick wools in a mixture of open-work and heavy straight stitches.
In the same idiom one could make a pattern of couched string and
give the cloth a macramé fringe.

Tea-cloths were different again. Tea was quite a ritual served in
the drawing room (where Algernon ate the cucumber sandwiches
intended for Lady Bracknell) or, in the summer, in the garden (as
immortalised by the Mad Hatter's famous tea party).

For all that Elizabeth Glaister thought white cloths so 'promiscuous' she allowed that a cloth for the tea table was a very good
subject for embroidery. She was keen on drawn-work, which she
surprisingly claimed could be 'easily' done. She also liked outline
designs worked in ingrain (which is any material dyed before

being woven) cotton or silks. She thought indigo and yellow were the best colours as they washed well. French marking cotton also met with her approval and the fact that it faded added, she thought, rather than detracted, from the effect. Silk was the best embroidery material because of its sheen and texture and because it was improved by being 'accidentally' washed out.

Crochet was very popular for tea-cloths (Plate 45) as was figured damask, left plain or its design unfortunately emphasised by embroidery and braiding, with matching serviettes (Plate 46).

While 'napkin' was correct for luncheon or dinner, 'serviette' was accepted for tea time. These were much smaller than napkins: left plain, with lace edgings, embroidered all over or given a design in one corner only, initials in raised satin stitch being thought very smart. Another tea table accessory was the cosy. A very rich one of the '80s was made of cashmere and given a 'Renaissance' design carried out in appliquéd and embroidered plush. Simpler ones could be made of crochet or machine lace. As tea gowns of the 1900s became frothier and frothier so did the cosies. Made of lace, ribbons, silks and embroidery they looked more suitable for the bedroom and were often referred to as 'lingerie' cosies. Others were more simply embroidered in the inevitable Edwardian 'Louis VI' style but even these were given fussy cords and tassels.

Mantelpiece hangings

As our redoubtable Miss Glaister put it: 'The fire-place being part of the room where for a great part of the year our leisure moments are spent and our affections chiefly concentrated, this hanging demands the most careful planning and the most exact workmanship.' Although early Victorian mantelpieces seem to have been

46 An 'artistic' mantelshelf valance, with a spray of appliquéd flowers, loops of cord and plush balls, 1889

47 Cloth mantle border, worked in silks in chain stitch and embellished with spangles and bugle beads, 1882

left bare, by the 1850s drapery had become quite general. As the *Young Ladies' Treasure Book* of 1853 pointed out: 'Mantel hangings or valances, have now become an accepted portion of household decoration.' If the mantelpiece were a 'work of art' in marble or wood, then it was grudgingly allowed to remain uncovered but if of a 'gloomy black, chilly white, or unsympathetic grey marble' then it was better to hide it with 'well arranged' drapery. No material was considered too costly to be either painted or embroidered (Plates 46, 47, and 48). Such was the Victorian horror of exposing anything, that some fire-places were given curtains or even completely boxed-in with material.

Such 'arrangements' were also given the name of *lambrequin*—a word which also applied to what we should call window pelmets, and to edgings for the shelves of bookcases and cabinets, wall brackets and even tables. Early ones were made of strips of scalloped or pointed Berlin work but it was not long before many other techniques were employed. In Tenniel's illustration of Alice making her way through the Looking Glass, the mantelshelf is edged with what looks like thick net, given a scalloped edge and trimmed with ball-fringe. This dates from 1872 and during this decade the most usual form of covering was to use a board (thick enough to prevent warping) which projected one or two inches beyond the shelf and was covered in material which hung over the edge to a depth of between six to as much as eighteen inches. If embroidered, the pattern took the form of continuous repeat or of a centre device with a matching pattern at either side. In the '80s black or crimson sheeting embroidered with gold-coloured silks in a scroll pattern and edged with cord and fringe was considered smart as was the use of gold or silver tinsel wool.

During the '80s and '90s very elaborate draping was popular

48 Felt machine-embroidered mantle valance or pelmet, c 1880

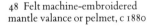

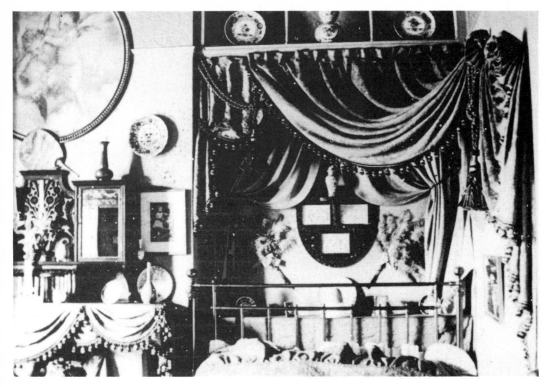

(Plate 49). But such a practice did not go uncriticised. R. H. Haweiss in 1880 disapproved of festoons of velvet as dirt made them unfit to be touched, as well as looking like 'dress-leavings'. She considered that muslin was the worst material of all and recommended a flat board which could be easily brushed.

Valances were considered very elegant and highly acceptable as presents. But would a bride *really* have wanted one made of white velvet, decorated with a wreath of orange blossom and leaves, intermingled with fronds of maiden-hair and given a heavy green and white silk fringe as well as a row of white carved wooden balls to make it hang properly?

In the Edwardian era, mantel-borders (as they were then called) were made of various laces, a typical combination being Spanish and Milanese. Spanish was easy to make as it was composed of braid joined by thick twisted 'bars'; Milanese was worked on net. These panels were separated by sections of white embroidered linen and the whole thing edged with Spanish braid.

Screens

An adjunct to the mantelshelf was the banner-screen, hung on a brass bracket which hinged out from the shelf itself. This screen

49 Detail of an 1890s bedroom, showing elaborately draped mantle valance and alcove behind the bed. Note the fringes, cords and tassels, often hand made

50 Small banner screen on a brass and wood stand. Silk embroidery on heavy silk with fluffy fringe, cords and tassels, c 1835

was to protect the faces of those who sat too close to the fire, and were usually made of Berlin work, often beaded and heavily fringed. There were also smaller banner-screens on metal stands (Plate 50) which must, for the same purpose, have stood on little tables.

As well as these small varieties there was the larger pole-screen, an echo of the elegant eighteenth-century ones which were usually shield shaped and covered in embroidery or fine woven silk. But such elegance was not to the Victorians' taste and their screens were made of heavily carved mahogany with Berlin work panels (Plate 51). Equally heavily carved and even more cumbersome were Berlin worked floor firescreens (Plate 52). There were also

52 Firescreen with Berlin wool-
work picture of Queen Victoria's
pets, her dogs Fido and Islay and
macaw. Taken from a painting by
Landseer, c 1850

small hand-screens, executed in Berlin work, or silk embroidery
on satin or perforated card. They were mounted on a wire frame,
often fringed and given cords and tassels; ivory being the favourite
material for the handles.

Several pole-screens were shown at the Great Exhibition. For
one it was claimed that no engraving could do justice to it. Which
was probably just as well as it was carried out in gold, steel, blue,
black, white, opal, grey-blue and green beads combined with
green and scarlet wool, lilac and crimson chenille and twelve
graduated pearl beads for highlighting.

By the '70s there was a taste for using ancient Japanese embroidery or old Venetian leather. But as these were acknowledged to be
expensive, less costly needlework varieties were available. Folding
screens of various heights and sizes were very popular—and neces-

sary. Large ones in the '70s could be covered in brown linen or serge and worked in crewels with a veritable herbaceous border of poppies, arum lilies, sunflowers, irises, hollyhocks and dahlias. Smaller screens were made of richer materials such as satin or brocade worked with lilies, roses and carnations.

In 1877 Whistler designed his famous peacock room for 49 Princes Gate in London. This exotic bird was to be adopted as the leit motif of both the Aesthetic and Art Nouveau Movements so it is not surprising that in 1880 a peacock with his tail displayed could make a splendid panel for a screen. It had to be conventionalised,

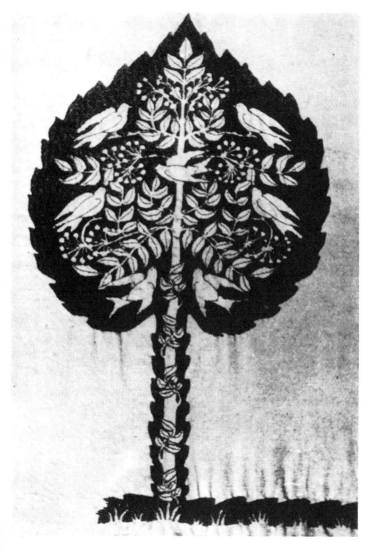

53 A typical Art Nouveau screen. Mainly in long stitch, unfinished, c 1900

54 A four-fold Art Nouveau screen. Silk with silk and gold thread embroidery, c 1899

and its colours reduced to the fewest, but even so, it might tax the embroideress's skill to make him gorgeous enough.

For those who thought a peacock too difficult a bird to attempt, then swans, cranes, flamingoes and ducks might be easier. Water and other surroundings had to be indicated with 'reticence, not attempting a pictorial representation'. (We are a far cry from 1850s parrots worked in looped wool stitch and 'shaved' to give a realistic effect.) Following Whistler's lead with his blue and white china, slender furniture and restrained colours, Japanese-inspired screens were very popular and could make a 'suggestive' picture, if care were taken not slavishly to copy the originals as their apparent disorder was a great snare to the unwary (Plates 53 and 54).

Despite the success of human figures carried out on screens by such well-known artists as Burne-Jones, these were considered unsuitable for amateurs. Not that this stopped them. As Elizabeth Glaister pointed out: 'Some terrible examples of failures . . . rise before the mind's eye and it should be remembered that to fail in so lofty an attempt as a classical figure, is to fall very far, and very ignominiously.' Poor dears, they weren't *trying* to be Michelangelos.

Many 'Louis Seize' screens were made during the Edwardian period. One could buy designs at 1s 6d a panel; three matching panels (already traced with the stitching begun in moiré) cost 55s. Such a design was considered 'so harmonious and delicate that the artist who stitched [it] may well have been a contemporary of Marie Antoinette'. The embroidery was to be carried out in silver-grey, grey-green, 'old rose', gold and white, and the ground could be sprinkled with gilt spangles. A pastiche, but an elegant one. Such panels were usually handed over to a professional cabinet-maker to make up into a screen with frames in a matching style.

Couvre-pieds

As the archetypal Victorian invalid Elizabeth Barrett must stand (or rather recline) supreme. One sees her (until released by Browning) forever resting on sofas, propped up by cushions and bolsters and wrapped about with rugs which the Victorians, ever slaves to the French language, chose to call *couvre-pieds*. Like other such objects they were often heavily embroidered.

For warmth (like a quilt) covers needed to be lined and wadded. They were made of patchwork, *Guipure d'Art* or other lace-like squares sewn together. By the '80s they were also being called 'small coverlets' and made of embroidered light serge, silk, satin and cashmere—although the latter was thought not a very good ground for embroidery. Thick satin Turkey (always scarlet and plain or twilled) was, on the other hand, considered a most beautiful surface, especially if sewn with gold, pale pink, blue and dark-red brown silks. Such coverlets were also made of alternating bands of blanket flannel and crochet. The flannel would be embroidered with flowers and the whole thing given a heavy silk fringe. Cricketing flannel or frieze (a material covered on one side with little tufts) being so warm were thought to be eminently suitable for those confined to, or merely resting on, a sofa. Even these materials would be embroidered in wools and given a knotted woollen fringe.

Scarves

These were not only worn but featured largely in interior decoration during this period. It was fashionable to fling a scarf over the

55 Scarves used for interior decoration: (*on the table*) embroidered silk given a lace and tasselled border; (*below left*) patterned cretonne and velvet ribbon, fringed and tasselled; (*below right*) India silk, the ends decorated with alternative strips of silk and velvet, each ending in a chenille pompom, 1889

back of a sofa, a table or a grand piano (Plate 55). Paisley patterns in soft colours were fashionable during the '40s and '50s. In the late 1880s a popular colour, called 'pumpkin', was decorated with appliqué pansies and edged with deep 'antique lace'. A small square table 'so prominent a feature in many homes' required a special type of scarf. It could be made of dark green plush with strips of pink satin ribbon at each corner, the ends being finished with green plush crescents. This combination of 'the shrimp of sea and the green of the ivy' was thought worthy of approval by those who recognised 'high art'. Even an ordinary white towel could be embroidered with sprays of leaves outlined in green. A bureau would look well if covered with a 'dainty-looking' scarf of narrow Turkish towelling, edged with three rows of different coloured ribbons. For a piano, a scarf could be made of felt, edged with fringe, heavy tassels and plush pendants.

Patchwork or joined ribbons were very popular and in 1889 one could choose from thirty-five different fancy stitches with which to join them.

It is worth quoting in full a little 'story' of this year, whose style and content make us realise that we are dealing with a period which, in many ways, is as remote from us as that of the Middle Ages.

> She had a little portfolio containing etchings of marine views to place where it would be accessible to inspection; she saw her opportunity and improved it. For a smaller sum than she would have to expend for the material, she had fallen into the 'Marine bouquet' folly; she had purchased a pretty brass easel, well made and securely mounted, though very airy looking. A piece of pale gold India silk cost a trifle more, and this she made into a scarf and fringed it with sea-shells, stringing them on strong silk, graduating them so that the largest shells of each strand came first, and regulating the arrangement to bring a tiny shell at the extremity. One end of the scarf was allowed to fall over a corner of the easel, the other to droop from the little stand which supported it, and on the lower shelf were placed some bits of coral and curious submarine growths. Who could fail to appreciate the harmony of the entire arrangement?

Who, indeed?

The Dining Room

As the *Young Ladies' Treasure Book* of 1853 put it: 'We enter the dining room and everything breathes of comfort and that repose which acts so beneficially upon the digestive organs when they are summoned into active service.' As there were not many opportunities for embroidery in this room, this repose was probably achieved. For luncheon and dinner in the 'best' houses white damask and matching napkins reigned supreme. As a writer of the '80s put it: 'If spotlessly white and ironed to bring out the beauty of the satin-like weave, unornamented damask is always beautiful.' Not that this injunction stopped many an eager embroideress. Cloths and napkins could be given borders or centres of white embroidery, lace and drawn-work; borders were worked in coloured silks and wools and even elaborately couched cord, as well as lace. Linen napkins were embroidered in white linen thread or given drawn-work borders.

In the 1840s dish mats were embroidered all over with beads,

56 Diagram of how to make a
Richelieu work and embroidered
doily, 1908

57 The finished result

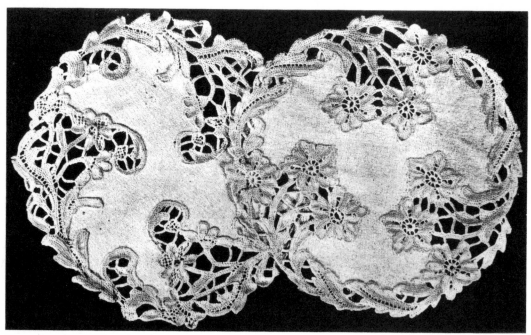

coloured initials on a ground of clear white beads being particularly popular. Doilies (which also appeared on the tea and dressing tables) also gave scope; they could be worked in broderie anglaise, in crochet and in drawn and Richelieu work (Plates 56, 57).

Cloths were needed for such things as bread baskets which could be made of crochet with the word 'Bread' worked into them, this stating of the obvious also being extended to fish and cheese cloths. One novelty was an 'Ornamental Meat Safe for Table Use'. The usual wire frame was ornamented with bands of worsted, embroidered in wools and given a deep canvas border worked in cross stitch. This object would probably have stood on an immense and elaborately carved sideboard which in its turn was given a cloth, decorated at the ends only, with everything from cross stitch to macramé.

Although in the very 'best' houses even silver napkin rings were considered vulgar, lower down the social scale they were much used, often being hand made. 'Silver' canvas rings embroidered in Berlin wool in two shades of crimson or old gold were thought very 'nice'.

Birth, copulation and death (T. S. Eliot)

The huge double bed dominated the parental bedroom. Here, all the numerous children were born; here copulation (which by *any* name was never mentioned in polite society) took place as did death, often in the presence of the whole family. So prudish were the Victorians about the bed's more unmentionable functions that a double bed was never shown in illustrated advertisements of bedroom furniture—even in the early twentieth century. *The Young Ladies' Treasure Book* of 1855 quite frankly admitted that 'We spend at least a third of our lives in bed, and care spent on making them [*sic*] comfortable is far from being thrown away when it results in procuring an added measure of "tired nature's sweet restorer, balmy sleep".' This 'care' included applying needlecraft to every possible surface, despite the admonition that in the bedroom 'as a rule we should avoid too great a variety of design in the decoration . . . at the same time beware of its becoming monotonous'. A dilemma which the Victorians and Edwardians seemed rarely to have resolved.

The parental double bed received the greatest attention. By the 1850s the four-poster was already going out of fashion to be replaced by one given a half-canopy. A very elaborate 'state' bedstead, shown at the Great Exhibition, is an extreme example of this style: made by Messrs Faudel & Phillips of London who had 'long been famous in their trade', it is a monstrosity of a bed, all 'classic' curves and draperies. The latter were produced 'principally from

British materials worked entirely by English-women in London' which included 'almost every description of ornamental needlework commonly called "Berlin" embroidery'. One would not find such an ostentatious example in even a well-off home but in 1837 many beds were still given a full set of hangings. These would consist of two large and two small curtains, valances round the base and one or two rows of tester (the overhead part) hangings. Even the headboards and tester ceilings and footboard were also covered in material. Very often all these pieces as well as the quilt would be carried out in patchwork—and an awe-inspiring sight it must have been.

At first thought it must seem that so much patchwork would have taken years to make. Until one realises that at this time no child, not even a boy, was allowed out to play until he or she had completed his or her quota of patches. As younger children were expected to make one rosette of five hexagons and older children even more, in a family of say at least nine children, it is not surprising that by the evening when all the patches were sewn together a large area had been completed.

Even so, such sets in patchwork were rare and patchwork was usually applied to only the quilt; often a wedding present and handed down from generation to generation. In 1880 Miss Glaister refers to quilts in the past tense so that by this time they must have been dying out. She wrote that 'perhaps no secular needlework gave our embroideresses more satisfaction, both in the making and when made, as the quilt or bed-coverlet'. She must have been referring to other techniques such as Mountmellick work, quilting and appliqué.

In the 1840s it was possible to knit a quilt in stripes of comparatively simple Double Rose or the more difficult Double Twisted Column stitch. In the 1850s joined-together crocheted squares were made in poor and middle-class homes. By the '70s it was considered that a bed-quilt would tax even the most experienced needlewoman more than bed-curtains and quilting itself was thought not worth the time spent on it. By this time it was more fashionable (as well as easier) to make a cloth coverlet (as it was then called) embroidered in a fairly simple branching design (as advised for curtains) enclosed in a border. Linen was thought to be the best material and for the embroidery silks, due to their durability, had the advantage over wools. For such a large piece of work it was wisely pointed out that one should start with a large stock of silks (or wools) because, if one ran short and the colours could not be matched, the whole effect would be ruined.

As a cheaper alternative, Bolton sheeting would do as well. This fabric, also known as 'workhouse sheeting', was a thick, unbleached coarse twilled cotton which improved the more it was washed. For embroidering, wool was more usual than silk.

Berlin work was even employed for bed-covers but as fine Java canvas was used they were comparatively light. One could even use a good quality linen sheet, divided into squares by drawn-work; each square filled with a different design in white or colours. If divided into four, the seasons could be represented: roses and sunflowers for summer; brambles and oranges for autumn; apple blossom and irises for spring; and holly and mistle-toe for winter. If one wanted to portray Day and Night, Labour and Rest, what more appropriate than sunflowers and poppies, peacocks and owls, the rising sun with moon and stars? And even verses from the morning and evening hymns.

Many joined-together towels made of huckaback, a mixture of linen and cotton, were also used for quilts, providing they were of a loose weave which would take running stitches easily. Macramé as a fringe or for insertions was used even for summer quilts but must have been rather heavy. For Irish quilts such as those in Mountmellick work, red threads could be used for the embroidery

58 A sheet end which combines drawn-work, crochet and an embroidered initial in a cartouche, c 1890

59 Pattern for monogram alphabet in 'Gothic' style, 1889

60 Diagram of how to execute an initial in a fine silk braid called Soutache, 1886

but the true Irish quilt was nearly always white. Most of the convent quilts made of linen, lace, crochet and embellished with various stitches were much admired and flooded English and continental markets in the 1890s and early part of the twentieth century.

By the 1880s eiderdowns were coming in and a typical cover would be made of *Guipure d'Art* bordered with swansdown puffs and satin frills.

Monograms and initials were an important feature of sheets and pillow-cases. Much bed-linen was part of the wedding trousseau and made of the best linen, the sheets being bordered in lace, crochet or other white-work often to a depth of two feet (Plate 58). For the initials there were many alphabets to choose from—from 'Gothic' to 'Renaissance' worked in raised satin stitch (Plates 59 and 60). Pillow-cases were usually square and often huge and could be orgies of drawn-work, broderie anglaise, darned netting, real or point lace and crochet (Plate 61). Initials also appeared on night-dress cases or sachets which were often more elaborate than the pillow-cases.

So much for the bed. It would be flanked by matching tables or cabinets over which embroidered watch-pockets were often hung. These were envelope-shaped and in the early days executed in Berlin work heavily encrusted with beads and given a thick fringe of beaded loops. There was often a matching larger pocket for 'odds and ends' (Plates 14 and 62). By the '80s such pockets were made of plush edged with lace or cashmere, appliquéd with silk and lined with quilted satin. Less ornate, as it was intended for the gentleman's dressing-room, was a wall pocket made of striped ticking. It was to hold his 'Toilet *necessaires*' but did not escape embellishment as the stripes could be embroidered with stars— light on the dark stripes, dark on the light.

The wife's personal domain was the dressing or toilet table. This was smothered in all manner of *necessaires*—some not all that *necessaire*. As well as the silver, ebony or ivory-backed brushes, combs and hand-mirror, the scent bottles and the candlesticks, there was a mass of other impedimenta which could be hand made. If the top of the table were not covered in a runner of Brussels or machine lace then a number of alternatives was available, such as finely embroidered thin canvas, crochet and embroidered or drawn-worked linen. There would be handkerchief containers or sachets in *Guipure d'Art*, often bordered with feathers; or a handkerchief box which was a mass of frills, ruched ribbons and lace. There would be a glove box—birds, flowers and butterflies embroidered on satin or a pattern outlined in couched cord; there might be a watch stand of black cane and embroidered Java canvas; there would be

61 A pillow-case in which several white-work techniques are employed. Darned net, inserts of needlepoint lace and satin stitch embroidery, c 1885

jewel cases; there would be crochet or lace mats for the candle-sticks; perhaps an embroidered and fringed scent bottle bag, or a toilet cushion (Plate 63).

There would be pincushions. These would be either for ordinary pins, hat pins, or be purely ornamental. Made out of silk or satin they were often wedding presents with the giver's name and date and a message such as 'May you be Happy' picked out in pins so that the object can never have been used. There was no end to the number of beaded, embroidered, patchworked, be-ruched, be-ribboned and otherwise over-ornamented examples, many made in the shape of shoes, mandolines or other curiosities (Plate 64).

In an age when even large households had no or few bathrooms an important item of bedroom furniture was the wash-stand which carried a matching china bowl, jug, soap dish and toothbrush holder. The marble top could be given an embroidered runner and the splashback—if not tiled—could be ornamented with an embroidered panel protected by glass. Bull-rushes and storks were a

62 A matching set of watch-pockets
and pocket for odds and ends.
Executed in Berlin wool and bead
work, c 1855

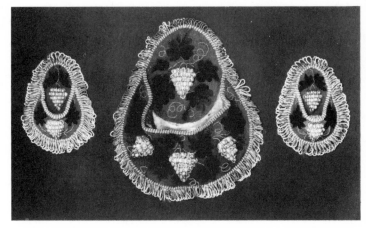

63 Coloured designs for a watch-
pocket and toilet or pin-cushion,
1889

64 Three pin-cushions in a sort of patchwork, consisting of scallops of felt, pleated and over-lapping. Two made to hang, probably by the dressing table, c 1870

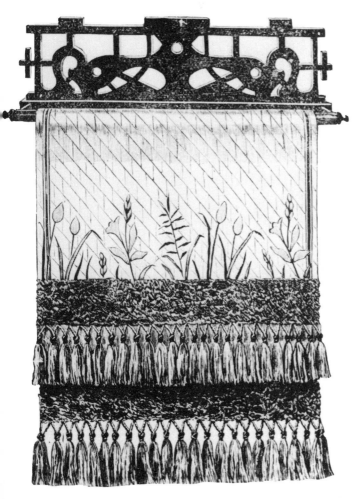

65 A towel-cover for a towel-horse. Made of linen with a band of Turkish towelling at each end finished with a deep knotted fringe. The linen is embroidered with 'selections from Nature's Garden', 1889

favourite device or one could make a panel of various laces mounted on a coloured ground; red Turkey material being considered a 'healthy' colour.

Towels were hung on the rails at each side of the wash-stand or on a separate towel-horse. These towels were made of anything from Turkish towelling to linen, cotton or huckaback. Most towels were given deep fringes of drawn-work, crochet and even tassels. Often a purely ornamental towel was hung over those actually used—the Victorians being ashamed even of their towels! This could be decorated to the heart's content. Coarse linen was thickly embroidered in cross stitch (a zigzag pattern being particularly popular) combined with lace insertions. Embroidered flowers and birds were popular, as was a 'towel' made out of different materials, the joins being disguised by feather stitch (Plate 65).

7 From top to toe

'All fineries are best new; new silks and artificial flowers, white gloves and white shoes, blonde caps and fly-away head-dresses, my daughter's muslins and my sister's satins, my boy's lace cornered cravat, and my own fine linen bands; not to mention the homelier things ranged in the wardrobe—the soft blue flannels for the rheumatics, the knitted woollen mysteries for the chill-blessed, the plush pad for the delicate of chest.'

THE ENGLISH WOMEN'S JOURNAL   June, 1859

As this is not a book on historical costume, this chapter will deal with only some of the smaller every-day (and night) garments and accessories which were hand or machine made in such profusion during this period.

The Ladies

Although C. W. E. Moberly in her *Dulce Domun* written in 1911 referred to the fact that her mother in the 1860s made her own close caps of Honiton lace, with lappets to the shoulders, because the fashionable shapes were neither tasteful nor simple enough, all manner of ladies' headgear was made of imitation and machine lace, crochet, knitting, netting and other techniques, some of them far from 'tasteful' or 'simple'.

For indoor wear, a cap or other head-dress was *de rigeur* up until the early '70s. In the early years as well as being made of lace, they were knitted in white Berlin wool edged with blue, pink or scarlet and interlaced with narrow satin ribbon. Wool was for winter; for summer one could knit a cap in cotton or make one of muslin, net or gauze, decorated with ruched satin or braid. By the latter years of the century, caps were even more embroidered, be-ribboned, be-laced and even feathered but worn more by the middle-aged and elderly than the young. The widow's peaked cap, *à la Marie Stuart*, is immortalised by the archetypal widow, Queen Victoria (Plates 66, 67, 68).

For going out in one's carriage, for a walk or for travelling by coach or train a comfortable cap could be 'easily executed' in crochet. For brown hair, the most 'comfortable' colour was considered to be yellow grading down to white. One such piece of headwear was called a 'Madame Rachelle's Travelling Cap'—after the famous actress. Rather daring was a vine-leaf cap. Its 'leaves' were made of velvet and the 'grapes' were simulated with

66 An Ayrshire work cap. Although made before Queen Victoria's reign the style lasted, in the country, well into the century, c 1820

crochet-covered steel rings.

For evening, a knitted hairnet in brown silk with a gold border (with as much as a yard of elastic to secure it) was smart in the 1840s as was a knitted opera cap. If more ambitious, one could knit an opera cape with a hood; if scarlet it was (naturally enough) called a 'Cardinal'. One great fashion leader was the beautiful Empress Eugenie, wife of Napoleon III. In 1855 one of the ensembles named after her was the *Coiffure à L'Eugenie*. This consisted of a head-dress with matching bracelets and had a success which astonished even the designer. It was 'so gay, so brilliant, yet so very elegant, and withal so becoming to everybody' that it was 'universally' approved of. The head-dress was made of a four-inch wide band of black filet lace, two smaller ones, a skein of cerise and one of *Vert-islay* silk. The bands were wound round the head and the four ends drooped low on the shoulders.

Caps were worn in bed, at the *toilette* and at breakfast—either very elaborate or mere scraps of lace and ribbon. By the more frivolous Edwardian era caps called 'Charlotte hats' were made to match embroidered summer dresses; they resembled eighteenth-century mob caps or the modern shower cap and were made on a wire frame covered with embroidered muslin and edged with lace. To be 'correct' the ribbon round them had to be tied on the *left*-hand side.

In the '40s and '50s necks were kept warm with ties knitted in fine purse silk and given fringes and tying cords ending in chenille tassels. By the '90s and early 1900s the number of high-boned collars and jabots was incalculable; they were mostly made of real, imitation or machine lace or finely embroidered muslin. One could knit a 'Vandyke' collar or a Berlin boa, or make a neck chain of the finest cut beads, threaded in bunches along skeins of fine purse silk.

No early or mid-Victorian lady went without her shawl. If not

67 The type of cap, probably a widow's, which was obligatory indoor wear, especially for the elderly, until the 1870s, c 1865

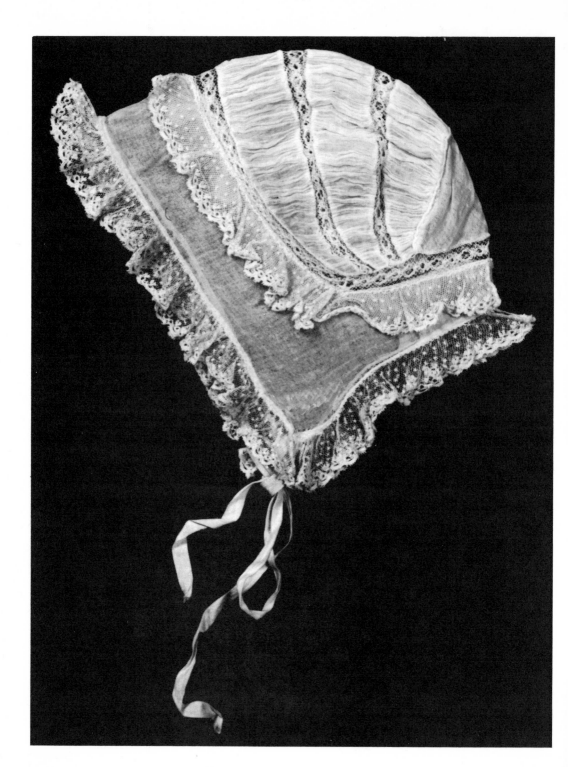

of the finest wool in Paisley pattern, it was knitted or made in crochet. Depending on the season it was made of double Berlin wool
or Strutts knitting cotton. It is amazing how *cold* Victorian ladies
seem to have been, for in addition to these stifling shawls (already
worn over a tightly fitting dress and masses of underclothing) they
often needed a small cloak-like garment called a Pereline, which
was worn *under* the shawl and could be knitted in three-ply fleecy
wool or made of crochet. As they were elastic they adhered com-
fortably to the form which rendered them an 'excellent defence in
walking or travelling in severe weather'. One imagines the Brontë
sisters clad in these serviceable garments when they strode the
Yorkshire moors.

One could also knit or crochet whole jackets called Spencers or
Polkas or, confusingly, Spencer Polkas. They were considered
'very superior articles' and had been very fashionable in the
lighter-clad Regency days but did not last beyond the 1850s.
During the '40s crochet was considered far superior to knitting and
one whose border, collar and cuffs were detachable and capable of
being washed separately 'without wetting the other part', was
much advocated. Even with all this, a woman (especially if unwell
or elderly) might be wearing a knitted chest comforter and knee
preservers.

68 Cap of muslin, trimmed with machine lace, c 1890

69 A muslin bow for a collar, trimmed with darned net, c 1870

Ladies could knit or crochet numberless collars and cuffs. Mrs
Warren's *Court Crochet and Cuff Book* of 1847 was only one of the
many books and journals giving instructions for these. Collars
could be *à la Greque* or 'Vandyke' and cuffs small and simple or
gauntlet-shaped. Many were made of Berlin work or consisted of
velvet bands sewn with beads. Sounding rather horrid, was a cuff
made of pink crochet balls, ornamented with short white bugle
beads.

For indoor wear knitted or crocheted mittens were much worn.
Ladies could also knit, crochet or embroider under-sleeves (Plate
70). A 'Spanish' one was in a concertina shape and would not interfere with fur cuffs but would 'effectively' warm the wrists.
'Bishop' sleeves were fashionable in the middle years of the century and could be embroidered, made of broderie anglaise or be
decorated with appliqué and edged with braid. Very like a
'Bishop' was the *Monquestaire* which, in 1855, was 'one of the
newest Parisian patterns which is worn more than any other style,
in morning dress' and was covered in raised buttonhole and satin
stitch flowers. The 'Balmoral' in crochet or knitting, was a series
of rather ugly balloons.

Muffs were very necessary in the cold out-of-doors. If not made
of material they could be knitted, or wool was used to imitate fur
for those who could not afford the real thing. Even in the '80s imitation fur was still being made. Saxony wool was worked on fine
Penelope canvas and the technique involved using strips of cardboard which were over-sewn with herringbone stitch; when the
centre line was cut, a pile was formed and the cardboard removed.
A good comb out and no one (it was fondly hoped) would know
the difference from real fur. By the '80s crochet was considered
'cheap' but a velvet patchwork muff could even be taken to the
theatre in place of the more usual handbag or reticule, to accom-
modate handkerchief, opera glasses and smelling bottle.

Women had carried bags for many years but the nineteenth century saw a plethora of them. Unlike her contemporary, the
Empress Eugenie, Queen Victoria was no fashion-plate. In Marshal Canrobert's account of her State Visit to Paris in 1855 he gives
an interesting and frank comment on her taste. Describing the
Queen's arrival at Saint-Cloud, the Marshal was struck by 'a voluminous object which she carried on her arm; it was an enormous
reticule—like those of our grandmothers—made of white satin or
silk, on which was embroidered a fat poodle in gold'. Unfortunately this 'voluminous object' was only too representative of
what many of the Queen's subjects also carried.

Evening bags were often less vulgar. A very rich bag (the design
of which was also suitable for a sofa-pillow or a counterpane) was

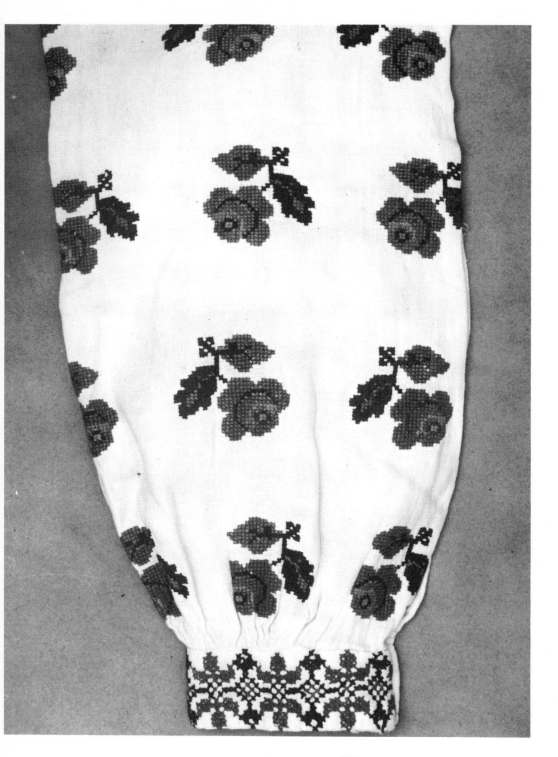

given a pattern of pines and Grecian scrolls worked in stripes of alternating colours. Silk bags were made of crochet with star-shaped bases. Velvet was decorated with beads or bags were made entirely of them (Plates 14 and 71).

By the '80s such objects were called handbags and more elaborately decorated. Embroidered canvas, on a foundation of cardboard, would be lined with plush and given a ribboned edging, or coloured silk in the shape of a small bucket was embroidered in crewel stitch and edged with cords.

Bags were not only for carrying. They could be hung over a chair or sofa, proving 'ornamental in a beautifully furnished room'. They sometimes held soft cheese-cloth which 'ladies' used to dust bric-a-brac too precious for the servants to handle.

There were shopping bags (plush and silk appliquéd with velvet) and knitting bags (which could be hung over the arm of one's work-table chair) and made of any material which took your fancy. There were also plush and satin bags in which to carry opera glasses.

Purses were as much used as bags. These, usually in a long sausage shape with a centre opening closed by two metal rings, were carried by men and women. They date from the eighteenth century and are now known as 'miser' purses. Made of fine netting, crochet or knitting they were patterned or sewn all over with steel beads as well as being fringed and tasselled. They were made in only one colour or in various combinations. One evening purse was made out of no less than twenty-three shades of crimson, three of green, and two reels of gold twist (Plate 14).

Throughout this period embroidery was applied to nearly every garment from day dress to evening cloak. As an antidote to the general *mode* it is worth recording some remarks made by Mrs Merrifield in her *Dress as a Fine Art* of 1854, in which she reveals herself as not only an early advocate of 'women's rights' but as possessing an 'artistic' attitude to clothes, long before the Aesthetic movement of the 1870s instilled its reaction to over-dressing and over-decoration. Mrs Merrifield was no amateur, being an Honorary Member of the Academy of Fine Arts at Bologna. She was also the author of books on art—a rare occupation for a woman at a time when such work was usually left to the Ruskins and the Morrises of this world. Opposed to bright rich tones, Mrs Merrifield was in favour of 'drab' or other 'quaker' colours. She disapproved of trimmings. Although she admitted that they were useful to mark borders their repetition only led to a stereotyped regularity. Above all, they were uneconomical, for as well as their initial cost they became shabby long before the dress itself and if removed left an unsightly mark.

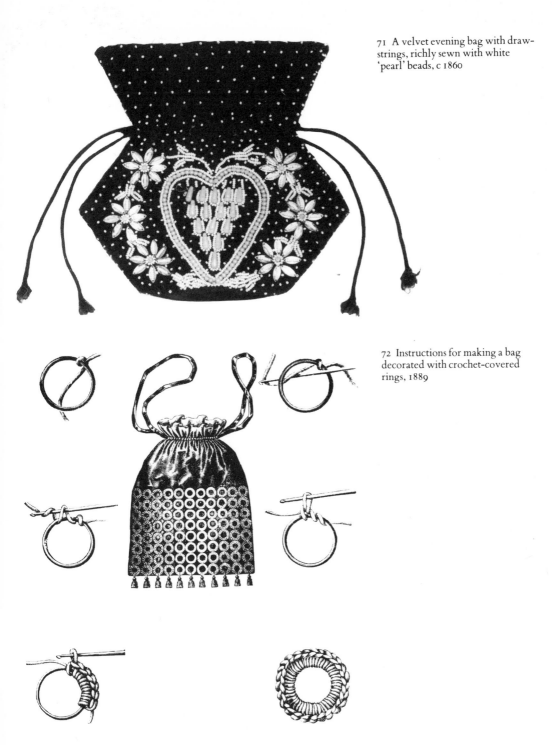

71 A velvet evening bag with draw-strings, richly sewn with white 'pearl' beads, c 1860

72 Instructions for making a bag decorated with crochet-covered rings, 1889

Other women's voices also strove to put their sex on to the straight (if often, boring) path of Health, Economy and Art as regards their clothes. In 1879 Mrs Haweiss published *The Art of Dress* in which she not only campaigned against tight-lacing but also had strong views about Economy. This, for Mrs Haweiss, meant saving on lace. However much you paid for it, it soon wore out, unless it were 'antique' when it would (she hopefully imagined) last for ever, however much it were cleaned or mended. She acknowledged that every ceremony of social life 'claimed its appropriate robes' because 'line, colours, textures, bear a certain affinity to human moods': sombre hues were for autumn and light 'sparkles' were for 'smiling spring', while the old needed 'rest' and the young 'a quiet rainbow'.

On a sterner note she was, even in 1859, all for Equal Pay. Seamstresses at this time earned only 2s 3d to 3s a day while a carpenter or house-painter could expect 4s 6d. 'What reason,' asks Mrs Mer-

73 A 'fancy' apron, knitted to look like Berlin wool work, c 1860

rifield angrily, 'can be assigned why a woman's work, if equally well done, should not be as well paid as that of a man?' Less realistically, she lamented that seamstresses' monotonous work left them no time for 'mental cultivation', ignoring the fact that most of these poor creatures would have been unable to, or incapable of, receiving this cultivation even assuming they had been given the necessary free time.

An example of one of the more silly of embroidered garments was the apron worn by ladies who profited from the labour of the under-privileged. Ever since the seventeenth century, ladies of the upper class, who had little intention of working, had worn decorative aprons. They were out of fashion during the Regency period but were revived in the 1830s when they were again made of lace, silk and satin, embroidered and trimmed with lace or jet and even knitted (Plate 73). In the 1860s they were rather small; in the '70s, often worn at the *back*, over the bustle. In the '80s they were made of crash or scrim and embroidered in the then fashionable crewel work. The Caulfield *Dictionary* does not mention them but in 1889 an apron was regarded as 'a fit companion to the work-basket . . . and much artistic taste is now expended on this garment to make it a bit of loveliness to the eye and a dressy contribution to the toilette'. There was no limit to the 'dainty fabrics and beautiful effects' which could be achieved with embroidery, ribbons, lace etc. In the late '90s and early 1900s when so many ladies presided at Charity Bazaars they wore special aprons which were enlivened with a little discreet embroidery.

By the '80s the New Woman was appearing, actually swimming (even if her costume would make a woman of today look overdressed at a party), bicycling, playing tennis and alpine climbing. For these sports special garments (sailor-style for the beach) could be given embroidered collars and cuffs and many tennis frocks were embroidered or laced all over. 'Mountain' costumes were thought (for some reason) to be equally suitable for girls and 'misses' (what we should call teenagers) as well as for ladies of 'small stature'.

Although the Art Nouveau Movement of the '90s had some influence on greater simplicity, no tea-gown, dressing wrapper, breakfast jacket or what was called a 'combing mantle', let alone the ubiquitous blouse, was worthy of its name unless it was smothered in enough trimmings to give poor Mesdames Merrifield and Haweiss a stroke.

As Paris was *the* arbiter of taste it is not surprising that *The Paris Journal of Fancy Work and Fashion* of the '90s and early 1900s should have been so popular in England. It is a mine of information, both in its text and illustrations. Referring to a typical blouse of 1908 the

text claims, 'You will find this charming trimming invaluable as a
means of transforming lawn or net slips into the most elegant
blouses during the summer.' For all their frothiness many garments
were thought smarter if the lace were as coarse as possible; and
what was called 'coarse relief' (embroidery worked in thick
cotton) was much sought after.

In 1886 Lady Alford made a rash (and, as it turned out, an in-
accurate) assessment of the future of embroidery as regards
women's clothes. 'The gown,' she wrote, 'of which the fashion is
in every sense imported from France, will probably never again be
the vehicle for home embroidery.' How wrong she was is proved
by the fact that well into the twentieth century embroidery patterns for gowns were to be found in countless journals and magazines. By about 1905, when the hour-glass silhouette was 'out' and
sheath-like dresses 'in', the long panels at front and back of these
dresses (as well as their trains) were fit surfaces for much embroidery. The *Paris Journal* of 1908 remarked that 'warm sunny days
have been reluctant to put in an early appearance this year' but
showed patterns for dresses for 'the holidays' to be made of linen or
cotton and embellished with insertions of anything from broderie
anglaise to Valenciennes lace to embroidery of flowers or True
Lovers' Knots.

Women have always been obsessed with ornamental underwear; even if it is never seen, it makes many women feel more
feminine. This period saw the frilliest and most elaborate of them
all; at a time when society encouraged femininity to a remarkable

degree, underwear was perhaps more ornamented than before or since.

Despite many campaigns against tight-lacing, Victorian and Edwardian corsets must have been almost as tortuous to wear as the famous Iron Virgin of Nuremburg, but their harshness was often disguised with laces and ribbons. Even for summer wear (when they were often called 'cache' corsets) they were still boned; the only concession to comfort being ribbon shoulder straps. Late in the century corsets were often concealed by 'covers' made of hand or machine-darned net.

In the early years of the nineteenth century knickers or drawers were not much mentioned but later they were freely shown in pattern books. Sometimes extraordinarily shapeless, they were given ornamental frills or covered with lace and/or embroidery. Even in the 1840s the chemise was quite openly referred to in books on dressmaking and in the '50s a chemisette—a sort of dicky—was thought 'nice' if it were inspired by a Paris model. *Weldon's Practical Underlinen for Ladies* left little to the (feminine at least) imagination. The carefully drawn and described garments in their pages were often given extraordinary names (Plate 75). Among chemises there was 'The Brighton' (how naughty); 'New Jersey' (suitable for anyone at all stout); and even 'The Cissie'. You could knit your drawers or vests in Merino wool—although probably only 'sensible' ladies did this. More elaborate were such garments as combinations called 'Alicia Drawers'. The description of one combination is worth quoting quite fully:

> This pattern is suitable for longcloth [a kind of fine calico, made smooth by having its surface singed in a jet of gas] trimmed with Madeira embroidery [which resembled broderie anglaise and was worked by nuns in Madeira and could be copied by English ladies] on fine linen or cambric and is cut with bodice front and drawers in one to which joins the back, while a small sleeve is also inserted . . . the neck can either be piped or hemmed previous to being trimmed with embroidery which is slightly felled on.

There were also knickerbockers called 'Melrose', 'Augustine' and (confusingly) 'Lady's Knickerbocker Drawers'.

Petticoats have a long history. From the sixteenth to the eighteenth centuries when they were seen in the front openings of gowns they were often elaborately patterned, embroidered or quilted but went to ground (or rather, close to the nether limbs) by the nineteenth. Early Victorian ladies could knit them (how *hot* these must have been—but no hotter, perhaps, than the traditional red flannel ones), and their weight was mercifully lifted when the crinoline frame came in. Petticoats worn under the bustle of the late '60s and '70s were given frills almost as elaborate as the dress which went over them. By the '90s, when the silhouette was slimmer, petticoats were referred to as jupons. In the early years of this century they were called underskirts and were often made out of nainsook (a kind of muslin) edged with a flounce of simulated Valenciennes lace.

The under-bodice was usually made of flannel or longcloth and thought particularly suitable for delicate ladies or those requiring extra warmth. Then there were camisoles—even in 1900 often looking remarkably like eighteenth-century corsets—or softer ones given broderie anglaise or open-work decoration.

Lingerie which was *meant* to be seen, such as nightdresses, dressing gowns, breakfast jackets and the like, were, if anything, even more elaborately decorated than the 'unmentionables'. Throughout nearly the whole of the period the nightdress was a voluminous garment which fitted closely at neck and wrist. It was heavily tucked, embroidered and decorated with lace or crochet (Plate 75). By the early 1900s some nightdresses were at least short-sleeved, so that the arms actually showed. Dressing jackets were made like little smocks and breakfast jackets often tied under the bust with a ribbon bow. For winter they were made of flannel or light cloth; for summer then in lined muslin, baptiste, piqué or fine lawn.

The Gentlemen

Although the Victorian and Edwardian eras saw men as the Masters, in comparison with the 'gentler sex' their clothes were sparsely ornamented.

By the beginning of Victoria's reign the golden age of embroidered male clothes was over, late eighteenth-century English taste and the French Revolution having killed it, except for Court and very formal wear. Although embroidered examples of waistcoats, called 'vests' (the modern contemporary American name for them) were shown at the Great Exhibition they were not worn by 'persons' of good taste. In 1855 black satin or cloth was considered the best material for a waistcoat, especially if decorated with coloured braid. A wedding waistcoat could be made of white satin edged with gold thread (Plate 76). There was an attempt to revive embroidered waistcoats in the early 1900s when small flowers or broderie anglaise were thought enough to satisfy 'the vanity of the sterner sex'.

Earlier the 'sterner sex' had been able to display a certain bravura by wearing embroidered braces, often carried out in Berlin

76 A cream silk waistcoat, embroidered in white silk, probably for a wedding, c 1850

work in a flowered pattern (Plate 77) or in an 'Ecclesiastical' Gothic design. Another item fit for decoration was the smoking cap. It was worn in (some) drawing rooms but more often in the privacy of the library, club or smoking room. R. Kerr in his *Gentleman's House* published in 1864 refers to the 'pitiable resources' to which 'some gentlemen are driven, even in their own houses, in order to be able to enjoy the pestiferous luxury of a cigar, have given rise to the occasional apartment dedicated to the use of Tobacco'. Even disapproving women made many such caps out of Berlin work, bead-embroidered velvet (Plate 14), patchwork, or covered them in braid or appliqué. A knitted cap (also suitable for wear in a railway carriage) would be carried out in

77 A pair of Berlin wool work braces, c 1850

stripes of claret, scarlet, green and blue, lined with silk and given a bullion tassel. Aware that such a bizarre combination of colours *might* embarrass a gentleman, even in the privacy of his various hide-outs, it could be executed in two colours only, which the ladies grudgingly admitted would look 'remarkably well'.

Slippers were another obvious surface for embroidery. In the Berlin work days and even long after them slippers were decorated in all sorts of patterns from the abstract to the pictorial: animals were popular but did not appeal to the logical and unimaginative Mrs Merrifield. She considered it bad taste for the head of a dog or fox to appear on the front of a slipper. 'How absurd,' she cried, 'not to say startling, is the effect produced by the head of one of these animals protruding from the trousers of a sportsman!'

Undeterred by such a consideration the ladies of England continued to stitch the offending heads on slipper after slipper. Many extant examples of slippers are not even made up, which led Margaret Swain in her *Historical Needlework* of 1970 to assume that slippers were unpopular. I think it just as likely that as slippers were often made as tokens of love, the loved one might have died or turned his favours to 'another' so that the poor lady hadn't the heart to make up the slippers even though the stitching had been completed. Slippers were also made out of crochet in double Berlin wool for morning (or 'undress' wear) or as overshoes. If for the former it was advisable to have them made up by a shoemaker but if for the latter, then a thick cloth sole could be made without recourse to professional aid. Very elaborate knitted 'Turkish' slippers were given cork soles but if intended for an invalid then knitted ones would be 'incomparably warm and soft'. Another orientally-inspired slipper was *so* elaborate that the designer of it in 1855 gave the following caution:

We trust that none of our friends will be deterred from attempting this beautiful style of work either by the grandeur of the name ['The Oriental'] or by an imaginary difficulty in gold embroidery. True, the most striking specimens of Oriental embroidery at the Great Exhibition [of four years earlier] were such as would require the wealth of a Croesus and the years of Methuselah, for any one person to accomplish; but the beauty of the embroidery was not better displayed in them than in the tasteful trifles which almost anyone may accomplish in the slipper.

If the task proved too daunting then the same design could be carried out on a smaller scale on a cigar case or a lounging-cap.

Men wore knitted cuffs; even mittens and 'comforters'; like

78 A 'crazy' patchwork man's dressing gown, each patch edged with fine cord. Signed and dated 1886

their women-folk they also sported nightcaps which tied under the chin. As well as 'miser' purses they could also carry the 'Imperial' (named after Napoleon III) made of scarlet silk with a gold clasp decorated with views of Paris.

The dressing-gown was a garment in which a gentleman could legitimately preen and parade himself. Very often of quilted brocade or velvet it could also be made of patchwork, either in a regular pattern or in crazy work (Plate 78).

The shirt also received a great deal of attention; for evening it was given lace frills and often embroidered; for day it was elaborately pleated and tucked. It gave hours of work to maids with flat irons and in 1850 seamstresses were paid only 2½d per shirt.

116

On the subject of men's nightwear one can do no better than to quote *Needlecraft: Artistic and Practical* of 1889: 'The decoration of the sleeping gowns of male members of the family is generally done by their home relatives, and the results are often elaborate and beautiful. The work is very simple, and not in the least arduous' (Plate 79).

The Children

Victorian children may have trailed clouds of glory; but most also bore the weight of superfluous clothing. As Mrs Merrifield put it in 1854 'Children are, by some over-careful but judicious parents, so burdened with clothes, that one is surprised to find they can move under the vast encumbrance.' Babies may no longer have been imprisoned in swaddling clothes, but those which they wore during the nineteenth century were, if not so restricting, almost as unhealthy.

Mrs Merrifield considered the age-long fashion for long petticoats for children—however prettily laced or embroidered—was as 'absurd' as it was 'prejudicial' to the child. She regretted that the 'evil of long skirts had of late years rather increased than diminished'.

These long robes continued to be worn throughout the century and the best and the most beautiful of them was the christening robe (Plate 80). Although at its best in the eighteenth century and at the beginning of the nineteenth, it was still a lovely object during most of the period under review. Like the wedding dress it was intended for a special, short ceremony and made with as much care, money and craft as the parents could afford—often, one imagines, beyond the parents' means. Unlike the wedding dress, however, it could be used more than once and was handed down as an heirloom. Those families with twins even had two of them. They were either lavishly made entirely of lace (Honiton being the favourite), Ayrshire work or embroidered or decorated with a mixture of hand and machine lace or broderie anglaise. Such a robe (and other babies' long garments) was high waisted and short sleeved, with a very long skirt. Its decoration consisted of a panel of embroidery, lace or ribbons beginning at the throat and widening to the hem: the same design even bordering the vast width at the base. In 1851 Sarah Anne Cunliffe knitted such a robe, using 6,300 yards of cotton to make 1,464,859 stitches!

Existing examples often strike one as being very small in the body. But during the nineteenth century babies were, on the whole, not only smaller at birth than now but were christened within days of their entry into the world—so high was the infant mortality rate.

After their brief moment of glory babies continued to be cocooned. As well as less ornate robes they were dressed in frocks—knitted (Plate 81), made of lace or crocheted. They were also given headgear of stifling thickness. Hoods often had fine Berlin wool knitted 'curtains' as well as being wadded, lined with satin and interlaced with ribbons. Even caps were trimmed with as many as four rows of lace or broderie anglaise, and for outdoor wear were topped with hats decorated with large feathers. Some babies' caps of the '50s were beaded all over on a crochet base; steel with emerald being a favourite combination. (For some reason, *grass* green was never used.) In the early 1900s bonnet-shaped caps

81 A machine-knitted baby's frock which was shown at the 1851 Great Exhibition

82 Baby's silk shoe embroidered in silk satin stitch with a ruche of ribbon, c 1860

were still being made of point lace or tatting, and decorated with embroidery or crochet. With their passion for making one idea do the work of many the same knitting pattern could be used for the base of a baby's cap, a doily, a toilet cushion and a round cushion cover!

Babies were given cloaks and neck frills knitted in double Berlin wool or three-ply fleecy in alternate rows of plain and open stitch. A muffler for a baby in the 1840s did not mean a scarf but a muff which was made with a 'thumb' and a ribbon with which to attach it to the wrist.

Then as now, babies' bootees or shoes were knitted, crocheted and embroidered (Plate 82). Then there were gaiters. Early ones were knitted and must have been easier to put on and take off than the cloth ones which the author remembers in all their stiff, buttoned-on horror.

Mrs Haweiss in 1879, under 'Nursery Hygiene' sensibly pointed out that drawers for children 'should be light and warm in texture, gay in colour, washable, never so expensive that a soil on it cost mother or child a spasm of the heart [Mrs Haweiss was expecting a lot of a child] and in form it should be regulated by common sense'. She nevertheless maintained that from babyhood children should be covered to the throat and wrist—the whole body being protected by light flannel—'not so thick as to wear and tire'. For all her sensible remarks her ideal child sounds incredibly overdressed; but one generation's ideal is certainly not another's. Today's almost naked children would no doubt fill the worthy Mrs Haweiss with horror.

Mrs Haweiss had more to say on the subject of children's hygiene. Aware of what previous generations of children had had to suffer she pleaded that no child should be forced to wear stays or corsets; even so, she advocated that the petticoat be buttoned to a warm bodice. By the '70s the hood had gone out of fashion so that children ('so liable to earache') should have their ears shielded out of doors as their 'useless' hats did nothing to help them in this direction. Mrs Haweiss was not against hats so long as they fitted her ideas. For her a 'capital' one could be made out of a 'mere' circle of cricketing flannel or marcella—which was a cotton quilting or coarse piqué—about three fingers in diameter and tied under the chin. It was simple to make, to fit, and to wash. It was a boon to nurses as it would never get out of place or 'tease the tender head'. Ever practical, Mrs Haweiss recommended using the 'leavings' from a home-made cape for such a hat and lining it with light silk.

Mrs Haweiss also had strong ideas about suitable colours for children's clothes. She favoured soft colours, quite rightly rejecting the fashion for deep plum with turquoise which was 'vulgarised in England to a mixture absolutely awful'. Unlike other over-optimistic reformers she added 'Alas! my countrywomen, the colour-art is not to be learnt in a day!'

Alas, too, her cautions fell largely on deaf ears. Even in the early 1880s children's corsets were still being knitted as were gaiters and what were called 'Infants' Polish Boots' in the most violent of colours. Mrs Haweiss might have approved of a crocheted turban-shaped hat and a 'Hyde Park Wrap'—the latter in crossed treble stitch. Reins had long been used to teach children to walk and keep them from straying. Called 'leading strings' in the sixteenth century and then comparatively simple, by the nineteenth they were elaborate constructions made of velvet or American cloth, bound with braid, embroidered and ornamented with rosettes and bells.

Sailor uniforms were almost *de rigeur* for boys and girls of the upper and middle classes. They were usually made of cloth but a sailor collar with scalloped edges could be made of crochet although as most children have a healthy dislike of the fake, they cannot have been very popular.

The garment most universally worn by all classes of boys and girls from about six months to twelve years was the pinafore. Worn to protect the rest of the clothing at work or play it was plain and serviceable for the lower orders or frilly and be-laced for the better-off. At the end of the century pinafores could be made in military or Indian style 'calculated to delight the juvenile heart'. In about 1900 a 'pinafore frock' was given a band of embroidery down the front to make it the very best of 'pinnies'. As with smocking and smocks, pinafores became so elaborate and over-ornamented that they were finally garments in their own right and no longer served their original useful purpose.

8 'Tiny fingers of the little child'

'Mary Fuge Gendle is my name
And with my needle I work the
Same and by my work you all may
See how well my Parents brought up me.'

SAMPLER   C. 1850

Although children of all classes were expected to be proficient in at least one branch of needlecraft there was one which they could call their own: that of the sampler.

Not that this had always been so. The sampler was originally a sample or record of a needlewoman's (or man's) stitches, and dates back to ancient Egypt. Samplers continued to be made by professionals and amateurs in some quantity from the sixteenth century onwards, although few of these early ones have survived. Gradually, however, they became the preserve of children; so that during the eighteenth and nineteenth centuries one finds most of them being executed mainly by girls from the age of six to sixteen. Until the end of the eighteenth century, even in children's hands, they were what they had always been: samples of work, but, as with so many an art and craft, their nature changed. By the end of the nineteenth century they were more of an exercise in needlework to be framed and hung on the wall, than a reference-guide.

Samplers were made in such variety, using such a multitude of stitches, designs and motifs that whole books have been devoted to them alone; enough here to say, briefly, how they appeared in the period under review. Few artefacts sum up the difference between the lower and the upper classes better than the sampler. Upper and middle class ones were principally decorative (Plate 83). They displayed such motifs as houses, trees, flowers, animals and birds (including peacocks), figures, ornamental bands and borders, carried out in many-coloured different stitches. They depicted what a child of this class was accustomed to see, if not always every day, then in illustrated books. These samplers would include a religious or sentimental inscription which, even for privileged children, reminded them that they were Basically Wicked, that Obedience was the greatest Virtue and that Life was Short.

A sampler made by a child at a village or Dame school, in an

In the sampler image:

Jesus is the one thing needful
I without him perish must
Gracious Spirit make me heedful
Help me in his name to trust

Esther Brown Her Work June
1842

orphanage or institution, is in stark contrast (Plate 84). It shows few houses or flowers and certainly no peacocks. It often consists of only an alphabet, numerals, the Lord's Prayer, a religious saying or rhyme. There was little variety of colours, the most basic sampler having only two. Often only cross stitch was used so that it was not really a 'sampler' at all but an exercise instilling hard work and humility. The more favoured of the lower orders were allowed the occasional fancy border and little house, which relieved the monotony of alphabet and humiliating text.

83 A middle-class sampler, finished by Esther Brown in 1842

Many people who collect samplers both here in England and America think of them as only charming and beautiful objects (which they often are) but forget that they are also the work of many a girl from stately home to orphanage, who must have longed for the day when she could complete her task with her name and the date.

Even so, some girls *must* have enjoyed doing such work. It is hard to credit that even so much eye-straining endeavour was not without its satisfactions. If nothing else, it gave girls an opportunity to show off and be praised.

84 A lower-class school sampler, worked in two colours. By Leonara Kate Henley, c 1860

Although eighteenth- and early nineteenth-century samplers carry religious inscriptions they were nothing to those painstakingly stitched by the end of the century which for strictness, sentimentality, high moral tone and bathos are not to be equalled. Typical is one by Sarah Duffin (obviously the inmate of an orphanage or poor school) who in 1839 sewed the following painful rhyme in blue cross stitch:

> May our young minds be taught to know
> To fear God as we ought to do
> And walk in the path of grace and truth.

This was mild compared to the longer verse executed in 1842 by Anne Britton of Cock Road Daily School—which must have been a rather 'superior' school as her sampler includes baskets of flowers, ribbons and even a church. This verse runs (the full-stops at the end of each line being typical of the period):

> Beyond these lone walls.
> Assembling neighbours meet.
> And tread departing friends.
> And new made graves.
> That prompt the secret sight.
> Show each the spot.
> Where he himself must lie.

Modern thinking on the upbringing of children would deplore such morbid thoughts. Perhaps rightly so, but given the conditions of the times it was perhaps healthier as well as being far more honest, that children should know about and recognise death for what it is, than, as now, being encouraged to ignore it.

Many nineteenth-century samplers performed such functions as teaching geography by means of simple maps or served as memorials to dead relatives, friends or well-known figures.

The Regency saw the swan-song of the sampler and by the Edwardian era it was so debased as to be worthy of little consideration.

By the end of the century samplers were being worked more on linen canvas than on pure linen and for the embroidery, wool was more used than silk. So universal had cross stitch become by this time that it was known as 'sampler stitch'. As early as 1845 cross stitch had been recommended as a suitable stitch for the blind—although it is hard to imagine how they achieved it. A Mrs Jackson advertised that she possessed the 'requisite apparatus'—whatever *that* was—which was 'not more bulky than that used by the Seeing'.

By the '80s the cats on cushions, the flowers in pots and the decorative borders (let alone the peacocks) were becoming motifs

85 A flannel school sampler,
showing various stitches and a
made-up pair of drawers, 1894

of the past. The best samplers were being done in schools but even some of these were copied from commercial patterns which no longer included the traditional signature of the embroideress, but that of the advertiser!

Two pictures of the Victorian era—one factual, the other fictional—equally reveal the two sides of the social coin.

By 1850 Government Schools of Design had been founded for 'artistic education' and work done by their students was shown at the Great Exhibition. Apart from these, the number of 'ordinary' daily or boarding schools grew steadily throughout the century. Most of them included the teaching of plain needlework which would equip lower-class girls for jobs in service, as housewives to earn a meagre living at home, as seamstresses in a sweat shop or to be teachers. As a sample pupil let us take Ellen Mahon who attended Boyle School in the 1850s.

As early as 1821 a Government regulation laid down that in the general arrangement time must be allowed for needlework. The syllabus for darning went as follows: 'The children to perform the work in two colours, blue and yellow, on linen that it may appear more distinctly. When a child has completed one of these darns she may practise on a small piece of muslin in which a hole has been purposely torn.'

Ellen must have been one of the more gifted children because in 1852 she was allowed to fill the whole of one of the cloth 'account' or sampler books which were regularly kept in many schools. Most girls were given only one cloth 'page' each (Plate 85). The first pages of such books resembled school samplers, done in cross stitch. Other pages were devoted to knitting, fine sewing, plain stitching and examples of gussets and gores needed in garment making. Crochet and patchwork were also included.

Teachers were issued with instruction books such as *Needlework and Cutting Out* published in 1884. It consisted of 'Hints, Suggestions and Notes for the Use of Teachers in Dealing with the Difficulties in the Needlework Section.' It was written by Kate Stanley, FRBS Head Governess and Teacher of Needlework at Whitelands College in Chelsea in London. It was dedicated to Professor Ruskin. In contrast to the fulsome prefaces in books intended for 'ladies', Kate Stanley wrote a brief and terse introduction: 'Within the last few years, Needlework has taken, and wisely taken, a much more prominent and important place than it formerly did in the Education Code.'

The first chapter of her book is devoted to Elementary Stitching. She did not approve of this being entrusted to pupil-teachers for 'unless a good standard be laid in the lower standards, they will not succeed when promoted to the higher'. The pupils had early to be made to avoid Waste. They were taught to make the necessary preparatory folds not in material, but in 'moderately' stiff paper such as pages from old copy books as the ruled lines would help the 'little workers'. The girls were provided with soft unbleached calico (cut selvedge way) and loose enough in texture to allow the threads to be easily counted; two coloured cottons and 'suitable' needles—by which the author meant those not so coarse as to make large holes in the fabric.

Now the 'little workers' could get to work. Apart from the techniques already outlined in the 'account' books they were taught to Make a Hem, to Sew and Fell a Seam, to Sew on Buttons (from Pearl to Linen), and to Attach Tape Strings. They were instructed in Gathering, Stroking and Setting in Gathers (which sounds like a quotation from *Alice in Wonderland*) as well as how to Patch Calico, Printed Material and Flannel. They learned to Make Tucks and to Execute Whipping (including Sewing on a Whipped Frill) as well as General Patching. General Darning included how to Repair Household Linen, how to Strengthen Thin Places and how to Darn a Triangular Tear and a Diagonal Cut in a table cloth.

Once they had mastered these skills and reached Standards V and VI as laid down in the Government Code, the girls could turn to Cutting-out and Making-up. Each girl, with the scissors suspended at her side, began work with an inch tape, a piece of soft, yellowish-white paper for making a duplicate pattern, a lead pencil, a T-square and a ruler.

Having been especially proficient with her 'account' book one assumes that little Ellen would have found the following operations comparatively simple. When she and the other children had been properly arranged the teacher showed them a specimen of the garment to be cut and then proceeded to demonstrate how it was made, explaining each step as she went along: 'I cut a piece of paper twenty-five inches long and twenty-seven inches broad and fold it in half length-wise'—and so on. These lessons taught the girls how to make Baby's First Shirt; an Infant's Barrow (a flannel garment which tied at the back); a Nightgown; a Long White Petticoat; a Robe (rather like a christening one) and a Pinafore for a Baby. They also learned how to make a Woman's Chemise and a Gored Flannel Petticoat.

Thus equipped, young Ellen and thousands like her would go out into a world which was only too ready to take advantage of her skills but less willing to pay a living wage for them.

The second picture is an upper- or middle-class one (Plate 87). It shows a fictional girl called Little Mary and her Mama. Mary was created by Mrs Warren and/or Mrs Pullan in their *Treasures of*

86 A baby's nightdress, decorated with broderie anglaise and machine lace. With a copy of *Needlework and Cutting Out* open at the pages of instruction, 1884

87 A typical middle-class girl at work on her sewing: a prototype of 'Little Mary', 1876

Needlework of 1855. Under the general title of 'Work Tables for Juveniles: or Little Mary's Half-holidays' it was a series of articles which gave instructions, by means of dialogue, for making a number of articles not included in the rest of the book. The tone betrays a typically spoiled middle-class girl who did not possess the attractive matter-of-factness of an Alice. (It is interesting that most of the more sentimental and tiresome children of Victorian fictional children were given the prefix 'Little'—such as Eva, Nell and Lord Fauntleroy. Mary was well up to their standard.)

These Half-holidays (from, one presumes, the governess's les-

sons) were devoted to Mary's desire to make presents for family
and friends. Much later in 1908 *The Needlework Monthly* confessed
that 'candidly, the time immediately before Christmas is somewhat a trying one' but it does not seem to have been so for Little
Mary and her Mama (or for Mary at least) fifty-three years before.

'Now my daughter, [begins Mama] if you are quite ready, we
will begin preparations for your Christmas Tree. See, I have
brought you down a box of materials of all kinds, which will be
indispensable for your work. I hope you will take great care of
them, for some are very expensive.'

'Indeed, I will dear Mama! How good you are to supply me so
well. Here are wools, purse-silks, gold thread—in short, it
seems to me you have thought of everything.'

'At all events, there are the materials enough to occupy you
for some time. But we must not waste your half-holiday in talk-
ing [They appear to do little else]. Have you resolved what to
begin with?'

'No, Mama; but it should be something very easy, and which
can be quickly finished. [Was Mary, after all, a *lazy* child?] I
should like to do some trifle of crochet.'

'Then suppose you make one of the miniature smoking caps
that are used to protect the burners of Hadrot lamps from smoke.
They look pretty, and are useful, also. If you work hard you'll
get one done in an hour or so.'

This particular object was to be made in white, black and blue
wools and steel beads, sewn on crochet. But Mary goes on:

'Can you not tell me of something else which I might be able to
finish before bed-time? What is that small round bit of cloth for?
[Neither Mary's nor her Mama's grammar was very good.] It is
too small for a mat.'

'It is for a pin-cushion.'

This was already marked out with a pattern to be carried out in
black, scarlet and gold embroidery. It was to have a fringe of bugle
beads and be topped by a plumed button.

As is clear from the following exchange on another half-
holiday, Mama was in the habit of making regular visits to Paris to
glean the latest ideas.

'Well, my daughter, I suppose you have been half afraid that I
should not return from Paris in time for your holiday. However,

132

you see I am here, ready for your lesson, and have seen so many new and pretty things, that I hardly know which to choose for you to do.'

'Pray let it be something very easy as well as pretty, dear Mama. I should like a work basket, or something of that sort which would be useful to grandmama, and look well on our tree besides.'

This basket was to be made on a wadded wire frame and covered with black satin decorated with black filet imitation netting and matching sarcenet ribbon. During another of their 'lessons' Mary proved a little *too* eager.

'I still want a present for a bride, and something pretty for one of my cousins—something she can wear. Besides—'
[She is rather sharply rebuked by Mama who replies:] 'For today, my dear girl, you have suggested quite enough.'

But Mama soon relents and refers to another recent visit to Paris when she remembers seeing a beautiful pin-cushion for the toilet-table. She says that she cannot recall it very well but is sure that Mary will like it. Mary cries:

'And that my new Aunt will like it too! Do, dear Mama, try if you cannot think of it. I am sure you will, if you search your brains sufficiently.'

Mama obligingly searches and comes up with a detailed descrip-tion which sounds perfectly hideous: in the style of an *Imperatrice* pin-cushion—named after the Empress Eugenie, it was covered in satin, topped with darned netting trimmed with gold and orna-mented with gold and silver passemeterie tassels.

'You will, [Mama assures Mary] find it very little work [she knows her daughter by now] and I think it should be admired.'

By way of giving the reader more information the child is made to ask the meaning of the word *passemeterie*, as her Mama is always using it.

'It is a French term, my dear, for that kind of ornamental work in which gold thread and coloured silks are worked up into cer-tain forms. You have observed that all the French purse trim-

89 A white silk photograph frame
embroidered in satin stitch, for the
Coronation of Edward VII, 1902

mings are of this kind, no steel or gilt ornament being used for them.'

And so on and so on. Thus were Mary and her like taught to make the thousands of over-decorated articles which filled too many middle-class homes for over eighty years.

90 A sovereign case in the form of a miniature book; the leather is tooled and the centre panel is petit point worked on perforated card, c 1850

Bibliography

Alford, Lady Marion. *Needlework as Art* London (1886)

Anon. *The Art of Drawn Work* New York (1901)

Anon. *Needle-craft: Artistic and Practical* New York (1889)

Anon. *The Young Ladies' Treasure Book* (1853)

Caulfield, S. A. and Saward, Blanche C. *The Dictionary of Needlework: An Encyclopedia of Artistic, Plain, and Fancy Needlework* A. W. Cowan (1882 and 1897)

Christie, Mrs Archibald H. *Embroidery and Tapestry Weaving* London (1906)

Colby, Averil. *Patchwork* Batsford (1958), Branford

Colby, Averil. *Quilting* Batsford (1972), Scribner (1971)

Cooke Taylor, W. *The Handbook of Silk, Cotton and Woollen Manufacturers* (1843)

Cunnington, Willet and Cunnington, Phyllis. *Handbook of English Costume 19th Century* Faber and Faber (1959), Plays Inc. (1970)

de Dillmont, Therese. *Encyclopedia of Needlework* London (1886)

Digby Wyatt, Sir Matthew. *Industrial Arts of the 19th Century* London (1851–53)

Doolittle, William H. *Inventions of the Century* W. R. Chambers (1903)

Eastlake, E. C. *Hints on Household Taste* London (1878, 4th ed)

Edwards, Joan. *Bead Embroidery* Batsford (1966), Taplinger (1972)

Glaister, Elizabeth. *Needlework* Macmillan (1880)

Glaister, Elizabeth and Lockwood, M. S. *Art Embroidery: A Treatise on the Revived Practice of Decorative Needlework* Macmillan (1878)

Gloag, John. *Victorian Comfort: A Social History of Design from 1830–1900* Adam and Charles Black (1961)

Grant & Griffiths. *The Lady's Album of Fancy Work* London (1850)

Haweiss, Mrs H. R. *Art of Decoration* London (1881)

Haweiss, Mrs H. R. *The Art of Dress* London (1879)

Higgin, L. (Edited by Lady Marion Alford). *Handbook of Embroidery* London (1880)

Hughes, Therle. *English Domestic Needlework: 1660–1860* Lutterworth (1961)

Jackson, Mrs Elizabeth. *The Practical Companion to the Work-Table* Simpkin, Marshall & Co. London (1845)

Jones, Mary Eirwen. *The Romance of Lace* Staples Press (1951), Saifer

Jones, Owen. *Grammar of Ornament* London (1856)

Keer, R. *The Gentleman's House* London (1864)

Kendrick, A. F. *English Needlework* A. & C. Black (1933)

Lambert, Miss A. *Practical Hints for Decorative Needlework* (1840); *My Knitting Book* (1843); *The Hand-book of Needlework* (1843); *My Crochet Sampler* (1844 and 1848); *Instructions for making Miss Lambert's Registered Crochet Flowers* (1852) John Murray

Lefbrure, Ernst and Cole, Alan S. *Embroidery and Lace* London (1888)

Lilley, A. E. and Midgley, W. *A Book of Studies in Plant Form with Some Suggestions for their Application in Design* Chapman and Hall (1895)

Longman, E. D. and Lock, S. *Pins and Pincushions* London (1911)

Masters, Ellen T. *The Gentlewoman's Book of Art Needlework* London (1893)

Merrifield, Mrs. *Dress as a Fine Art* London (1854)

Morris, Barbara. *Victorian Embroidery* Herbert Jenkins (1970)

Morris, May. *Decorative Needlework* London (1893)

Morris, William. *Hints on Pattern Making* London (1881)

Orrinsmith, Mrs. *The Drawing-Room, its Decoration and Furniture* London (1878)

Owen, Mrs Henry (Edited by the Countess of Wilton). *The Illuminated Book of Needlework* London (1847)

Proctor, Molly G. *Victorian Canvas Work, Berlin Wool Work* Batsford (1972)

Risley, Christine. *Machine Embroidery* Vista Books (1961)

Ruskin, John. *Stones of Venice,* Vol II London (1853)

Ruskin, John. *On the Present State of Modern Art,* Works (1871)

Sandford, Mrs R. H. *Woman in her Social and Domestic Character* London (1837)

Santina, Levy. *Discovering Embroidery in the Nineteenth Century* Shire Publications (1971)

Savage. *Needlework, Knitting and Crochet* London (No date, c 1845)

Short, Eirian. *Introducing Macramé* London (1970)

Stanley, Kate. *Needlework and Cutting Out* London (1884)

Swain, Margaret. *Historical Needlework* Barrie and Jenkins (1970)

Symonds, Mars and Preece, Louisa. *Needlework Through the Ages* Hodder & Stoughton (1928)

Symonds, R. W. and Whineray, B. H. *Victorian Furniture* Country Life (1962)

Townsend, Mrs B. *Talks on Art Needlework* London (1883)

Waring, J. B. *Masterpieces of Industrial Art* London (1863)

Warren, Mrs Eliza. *The Court Crochet Collar and Cuff Book* Ackerman & Co (1847)

Warren, Mrs Eliza and Pullan, Mrs. *Treasures of Needlework* Ward and Lock (1855)

Warren, Mrs Eliza and Pullan, Mrs. *Fancy Work Designs* Ward & Lock (1869)

Whitaker, Henry. *House Furnishing, Decorating and Embellishing Assistant* London (1847)

Wilton, Countess of. *Art of Needlework* London (1840)

Yapp, G. W. *Furniture, Upholstery and Household Decoration* London (1878)

Periodicals

The Lady's Newspaper (1847–1863)

Journal of Design and Manufacturers (1849–1851)

The Englishwoman's Domestic Magazine (1852–1879)

The Art Journal (1849–1912)

The Needle (1852–1855)

The English Woman's Journal (1858–1863)

The Ladies Treasury (1858–1869)

The Queen (1861–)

The Young Ladies Journal (1864–1920)

The Young Englishwoman (1865–1887)

Myra's Journal of Dress and Fashion (1875–1912)

The Girl's Own Annual (1878)

Sylvia's Home Journal (1878–1891)

The Lady's World (1886–1887)

The Woman's World (1887–1890)

The Studio (1894–)

Needlecraft Practical Journal (1900–1907)

Needlecraft Monthly (1907–1913)

Paris Journal of Fancy Work & Fashion (1908–1916)

Weldon's Practical Journals

Catalogues

Official Catalogue of the Great Exhibition of the Work of Industry of All Nations (1851)

The Art Journal. Special Issue. The Crystal Palace Exhibition Illustrated Catalogue (1851)

Catalogue of Exhibition of Embroidery, Ancient and Modern, Liverpool Art Club (1875)

Catalogue at South Kensington, Royal School of Art Needlework (1879)

Index

Numerals in italics indicate plate numbers.